The classic guide
to boxing

The
CLASSIC
GUIDE
TO BOXING

The
CLASSIC
GUIDE

TO BOXING

THE AMERICAN
SPORTS PUBLISHING
COMPANY, 1917

AMBERLEY

This edition first published 2015

Amberley Publishing
The Hill, Stroud, Gloucestershire, GL5 4EP
www.amberley-books.com

ISBN 978 1 4456 5100 2 (print)
ISBN 978 1 4456 5101 9 (ebook)

British Library Cataloguing in Publication Data.
A catalogue record for this book is available from the British Library.

Typesetting by Amberley Publishing.
Printed in Great Britain.

Contents

Editor's Note	7
How To Box	9
The Science of Boxing	29
Hints On Training	91
The Way to Hit	99
Rules Of Boxing	103

Editor's Note

Boxing has a varied and long history and is one of the most well known of contact sports. It was a major spectator sport in ancient Rome and more often than not was a fight to the death, which is a far cry from today's version of boxing. Boxing has certainly changed since then and evolved between the sixteenth and eighteenth centuries before becoming what we now know as modern boxing.

From the arenas of ancient Rome to modern-day bouts, a boxer's success has been measured by his balance, strength and recovery. One of the things that *The Classic Guide to Boxing* teaches us is that boxing is not just a sport but a science. Judging distance, position, arm movement and fist shape all contribute to a boxer's overall performance in the ring, and are spread out in informative chapters for improving amateurs. This handy guidebook also teaches its readers the art of performance, detailing how to trick one's opponent into being caught off guard, so that they can deliver the winning blow.

This volume was originally published by The American Sports Publishing Company as *Boxing: A Guide to the Manly Art of Self Defence, giving accurate instructions for becoming proficient in the Science of Boxing* in 1917. It discusses the essentials of learning how to box with some handy notes on defence tactics and cross-counter moves such as the 'Famous Solar Plexus Knockout' or the 'McCoy "Corkscrew"' that any enthusiast will appreciate. It also recounts the many rules of a boxing match. Relating notable matches between boxers including Les Darcy, Jimmy Clabby and George Chip, the book showcases the sport in its early glory days.

The Classic Guide to Boxing is a remastered version of this seminal work and is essential reading for anyone interested in the sport.

Vanessa Le, MA
Editor

How To Box

THE CORRECT POSITION

The first thing to be considered when learning to box according to latest methods is a proper and easy position on your feet. This point, in fact, should be given fully as much attention as active attack and defence, and no person can hope to become proficient in the 'manly art' that does not devote considerable time to perfecting himself along this line. Many of our leading exponents of the science of boxing have attained their prominence not so much through weight and brawn as through their superb generalship and footwork, enabling them, oftentimes, to offset an advantage of from 20 to 30 pounds in weight held by their opponents. The graceful carriage of boxing devotees is largely, if not wholly, due to the manipulation of their feet and legs while sparring, and besides this attribute they have gained strong, well-developed, though not necessarily large, muscles in their lower limbs. The circulation of the blood also has become wonderfully improved giving a buoyancy to the step which cannot have otherwise than a beneficial and stimulating effect on the entire system.

To take the correct attitude, place your left foot in advance of your right anywhere from 10 to 20 inches, according to height and length of leg. It is necessary at all times to maintain a perfect balance, dividing the weight equally on both feet.

With the feet too close together you cannot get full force into a blow and you are easily carried off your feet by a sudden attack; with the feet too far apart the inside leg muscles are strained and you will find yourself unable to move quickly in any direction to take advantage of an opening or to evade a rush. The left foot should be placed flat on the floor, pointing straight out in front to your opponent's left. The right should be placed directly behind the heel of the left pointing outward at an angle varying from 60 to 70 degrees. The right heel should be raised from the floor at least an inch, giving an opportunity to move quickly in any direction on the ball of the foot.

THE HANDS

The left hand is the boxer's main dependence. It should be held toward the adversary's chin in an easy position, with the palm turned slightly upward so that the knuckles will take full effect. The elbow should be extended at varying distances from the body according to the opponent's height. The left arm should be worked freely, avoiding a pronounced contraction of the muscles. The right hand is best placed across the body, the elbow covering short ribs, the forearm turned slightly forward, covering the pit of the stomach, and the fist being placed over the heart. The right shoulder is usually depressed several inches. In delivering straight blows do not permit the wrist to bend, and clinch the fist tightest at the exact moment of landing.

CLINCHING THE FIST

I consider it of the utmost importance that every boxer should learn the right method of doubling the fist. Even championship holders are deficient in the knowledge and practice of this feature of self-defence, and in my correspondence school I never fail to impress on the minds of my pupils the great value of observing definite instructions which will serve to prevent many painful injuries to the hands and fingers. Dislocated joints and broken bones are frequently reported in contests in which the best boxers of the land appear, and these accidents can invariably be avoided by a little caution and remembering that an ounce of prevention is worth more than a whole medicine chest of cures.

In closing the fist bring the tips of the fingers well over the palm with the thumb turned inside and over the first joint of the index finger, which will prevent the point of the thumb from coming in contact with the opponent's guard.

Relative to the poise of the body in action I would suggest that the pupil stand about quarter exposed. Do not present a full front to your opponent, but rather turn slightly from the waist, inclining the shoulders a bit forward. Let the body work freely, not loosely, with the arms and hands showing agility in every move. A contraction of the body muscles is very tiring and not conducive to speed.

THE ART OF GAUGING DISTANCE

Taking distance is the science of ascertaining as to whether or not you are in reach of your opponent while in action. Every boxer has an individual attitude calculated to deceive his combatant regarding his actual distance from him. Some there are that incline forward from the waist, giving the idea that they are in closer range than is really the case. This becomes plainly evident in leading at them. The followers of this style frequently drop into a natural position by throwing back the chest and shoulders, sometimes varying the manoeuvre by stepping back with the right foot a few inches, allowing the greater part of their weight to rest thereon. Thus they cause many a well-directed blow to fall short and at the same time draw a man off his balance. Others there are that bend back from the waist, creating the impression that they are farther away than they actually are, luring their opponent into dangerously close quarters. In taking distance be careful not to get in so close that your hands and those of your opponent conflict. Do not indulge with him in hitting the left hands together as you face each other, after the fashion of many novices. This is a waste of time and energy, serving no good purpose and spoiling the appearance of a contest. Distance gauging is invariably necessary in sparring for an opening and when doing this work to your opponent's left as much as possible, keeping out of direct range of his right until the time arrives when you can step in and lead.

THE FIRST PRINCIPLES OF HITTING

The primary motive in taking boxing lessons is to learn how to hit, to deliver successfully a blow to some part of an opponent's anatomy and at the same time avoid a return. Before

going into the details of the various blows I will give a few words of general advice regarding this all important feature. Always endeavour to step in and strike as quickly as possible, making the blow clean cut and decisive. The quicker the blow, the more disconcerting it will be for your opponent and the letter you will be able to recover yourself for another attack. Avoid, as far as possible, too many preliminary moves before actually striking. Feinting is all right in its place, but don't 'telephone' the nature of your blow by 'fiddling' nervously at the point on which you wish to land. Get your whole weight and power into your blows without pitching yourself off a wellbalanced poise and always hold yourself in readiness to follow up an advantage with a rush when circumstances make it advisable. A well-directed shower of blows backed by the momentum of the body often brings a victory, but the attacker should keep his wits about him or he may run into a knockout. A light man should not resort too often to rushing tactics in opposing a heavier boxer, whereas many a heavy man frequently gains distinct advantage by repeatedly rushing an adversary of lighter weight.

Do not feel that it is your duty to knock a man off his feet with every blow. Have system in your attack, reserving your supreme efforts for good openings. Don't put your full force into a blow which you feel will be easily blocked or pushed aside. Pay careful attention to the position of the hands and arms and keep the muscles relaxed when not in actual use. Seldom imitate the slugging style in hitting. The scientific boxer never indulges in the frequent use of the wild swings ('haymakers') affected by some pugilists, which leave you wide open to attack, especially when you fail to land. The clever glove manipulator would a thousand times rather get through an opponent's guard by generalship than by breaking down his guard by brute force. It is not advisable for boxers, especially beginners, to pay too much attention to fancy blows. The simple moves should be mastered first and then there is ample opportunity to develop those more involved. The lessons should be graded just as school studies, the pupil going upward step by step as improvement warrants.

THE ELEMENTS OF DEFENCE

Guarding the body is a most valuable feature of boxing which is seldom done entire justice by writers on the 'manly art'. In my classes I always lay particular stress on this branch of the science, informing my pupils that they should not devote too much attention to hitting, but should take great care to learn to protect themselves quickly and effectively from attack. In posing for the photographs reproduced in this book I took particular pains to bring out the guards for different blows, and careful observers are sure to derive much benefit from them.

Guarding comprises several distinctly separate moves, the principal ones being blocking, slipping, shoving blows aside, 'ducking', delivering 'stop' blows and side stepping. Blocking is unmistakably the first in importance and the most frequently adopted means of meeting a lead. A quick eye is a first-class aid as also is the faculty of divining in a measure your opponent's intentions, which some boxers have cultivated to a high degree. A block may be executed by interposing between the attacking fist and your body, the hand, the forearm, the elbow or the upper arm, as conditions render expedient. While guarding yourself in this way take care to keep an eye alert for openings which may offer a chance to land effectively with your free hand. Blocking should be done with as little effort as possible in most cases, but when an adversary puts considerable force into his blow it is advisable to meet it with sufficient power to prevent your guard from being driven back into your face or body. At the same time you will find decided benefit in giving way to the blow by swaying the body backward with the guarding hand well in touch with the blow, thus robbing it of its intended force. The right or guarding arm should not be allowed to go too far from the body, working inside the line of the left elbow, and do not reach out with it for a coming blow, for you will leave yourself unprotected.

Slipping consists in moving the body or head quickly to either side to avoid a lead or counter. In this way the hand of your opponent brushes by harmlessly. The head slip is very useful in avoiding right and left leads for the chin and face. To slip a right lead for the head incline the body slightly forward and turn the head quickly to the right, causing your opponent's hand to glide harmlessly over the left shoulder or to strike the back of the neck or skull a glancing blow. The slipping of a left lead is, of course, performed by turning the head smartly to the right.

In shoving a blow aside from its intended course you push your opponent's forearm to one side before the blow lands. This is done with either the hand or forearm, and with which the attacking hand is made harmless by forcing it wide and often throwing the attacker off his balance. There are also cases when your antagonist's elbow is pushed, your hand hitting the outside of his arm, forcing him to pivot around according to the arm shoved. The left hand is generally used for shoving, the palm and forearm being preferably turned outward. As in blocking, the opened flat of the palm can be put to good use in shoving.

Ducking is in many ways similar to slipping, being practically a variation of the latter. This movement is usually a forward one although right and left 'ducks' are of frequent occurrence in action. The 'duck', to be performed successfully, must be quick and the head must be kept well-guarded with either the right or left arm across the face to protect against a possible uppercut. The 'duck' is used in avoiding swings for the head and I strongly advocate striking a blow for the body with almost every move of this kind, for when yon opponent is leading high he often leaves an opening below. This sort of a blow is also very disconcerting because of the swiftness with which it is delivered. In 'ducking' forward guard the face and lead with either hand and lead to the body with the free one, holding yourself in readiness to spring back or to straighten up to send either the right or left across to the head.

The 'stop' is a blow delivered as an opponent prepares to lead or immediately after he leads, his blow having not yet reached you. This manoeuvre is a strong point in counter striking, which in addition to stops, includes prop blows and all counters. A boxer's success depends largely on his ability in countering and it should be the ambition of every beginner, as well as of the more advanced, to excel in this branch of the sparring science. Stops are invariably executed with the left hand to your combatant's head or body. Watch him closely and just as his eye, expression or attitude cause you to believe him about to lead, shoot out the left to land hard, beating him, as it were, 'at his own game'. In 'stopping' a blow, guard the face with the right forearm and draw the stomach well in.

Side stepping is always pleasing to spectators and it is an extremely useful element in a bout. It is generally brought into play in evading a rush or in getting out of a corner after you have drawn a lead. The side step is best executed by stepping back with the right foot, drawing the left toe back, placing it directly behind the right heel and in a straight line with it, and facing to the right, taking a long, quick step with the right. Then follow up with the left and turn, facing your opponent in boxing attitude. The different parts of the side step should be done so quickly as to become one complete movement, the impetus gained by the original spring carrying you into a position identical with that you first held.

FEINTING: AN INVALUABLE FEATURE OF BOXING AND HOW PERFORMED

There is not a single boxer in the land that does not appreciate the great value of a judicious feint. The practice of feigning a blow in order to draw an opponent off his guard, leaving an opening to attract him into a lead or to disguise the nature of an intended lead, is of universal usage and every able boxer places it close to the top of his list of accomplishments. Feinting is a predominating feature in every scientific bout and every boxer should make it a rule to feint once or twice before leading. Probably the leaders in this branch of the 'manly art' are Corbett, McCoy and Tommy Ryan. They are little short of marvels in this respect, having mastered it completely, if it is possible for any man to do so. Spectators at matches in which they have figured will readily affirm this statement.

The keynote of successful feinting is rapidity. Always bear this in mind. And don't be indecisive. Make up your mind quickly and start right in to suit the action to the thought. The correct feint is done as follows: Step in with the left foot around 6 inches, following up with the right foot. Straighten the left arm as in leading, sending the hand as close as possible to your adversary's head or body without touching. Retract the arm like a piston rod, with the muscles relaxed, and then to deliver the actual blow step in quickly from 8 to 12 inches, following up the left foot with the right to cover the former position of the left and lead the left hand sharply to any unguarded spot.

Feinting is generally called into play before straight leads to the head and body and the left hand is the factor most frequently employed. When it is desired to send the right or left to the face, feint low with the left as though to land it on the ribs or in the solar plexus – the uppermost part of the stomach, directly below the sternum, or breastbone. The opponent will naturally seek to block this blow and in so doing will be compelled to bring down all or part of his guard, leaving his face more or less exposed for an attack. At the same time you must remember to guard your own face with the free hand, your head being turned partly to either side, to the right when leading with the left, and to the left when using the right, but not so far that you cannot watch every move of your opponent. When contemplating a lead for the body feint for the face, thus drawing your opponent's guard high, guarding yourself and sending in the blow in the manner described in the preceding sentences.

Feints are made of particularly good use in drawing a lead from an opponent when he would rather remain on the defensive and they are very worrisome to a nervous man. The rapid changes of position keep him constantly guessing as to what is coming next. In some cases the arm need be but partially straightened and oftentimes a simple bringing forward of the shoulder, accompanied by a slight forward movement of the hand will serve to disconcert your combatant, as also will a brief backward jerk of the hand. A swift forward bend of the head can also be worked into a feint to advantage. The successful feinter invariably uses considerable foot work, stepping forward, backward, to the right or to the left, keeping his arm in motion. Care should be observed in preserving an easy balance so as to facilitate recovery in all instances.

Summed up as a whole, feinting is one of the prettiest, most spectacular, and at the same time very effective attributes of boxing and it is a direct advance over the methods of the old-time slugging school, the hammer and tongs, 'knock 'em down and drag 'em out' brand.

KNOCKOUT BLOWS

The Chin Punch
In reading and talking about boxing one hears a great deal about 'knockout blows'. The nature of these blows is accurately described by their title. A 'knockout' is a punch that renders a man unable to face his opponent for ten seconds or more and it can be delivered in various ways to various points of his anatomy. A knockout is generally delivered to one of four points: in the pit of the stomach or solar plexus, under either ear, affecting the base of the brain and over the heart. Most knockouts occur from the blow to the chin. 'The point of the chin' is usually described as the landing place of a

knockout of this sort but in reality it is not to the point but rather to either side of the exact point that the blow strikes. This is not noticed by many people but it is nevertheless true that few knockouts reach the extreme end of the lower jaw.

From everyday descriptions it would seem to the uninitiated that knockouts delivered to the chin are very painful and that they are of long lasting effect, but on the contrary the blow deadens the senses completely, making it impossible to feel pain or realize your condition. A knockout is as good an anxsthetic as ether or gas. The suddenness of the punch, which is not necessarily one of terrific force, is greatly responsible for the knockout, causing the upper part of the jaw bone to jar the brain. Beyond feeling a slight shock, a man struck in this manner knows nothing until he begins to recover, when he hears a low buzzing and all sounds seem distant. The counting of the referee and the commotion of the audience appear to draw nearer as his consciousness returns. In a few seconds he is on his feet again and if well trained he is very little the worse physically for his encounter.

The Blow Under The Ear
The blow under the ear is not a clean-cut knockout. It befol the brain and a man will stagger before falling. After his legs wobble

from under him, he may regain his feet in five or six seconds. An experienced man will invariably stay down for full nine seconds in order to recuperate as much as possible. The novice in his enthusiasm is prone to scramble to his feet as soon as he is able, regardless of consequences, and rushes wildly a his opponent, hardly knowing what he is doing, only to meet another blow which is easily landed on a man in his weak condition.

The Famous Solar Plexus Knockout

The knockout to the pit of the stomach, better known as the solar plexus blow, is distinctly painful. You do not lose consciousness but you find yourself absolutely helpless, doubled up as though stricken with violent cramps and unable to resume action. Oftentimes a man will sink to the floor with one knee and in a few moments the other will follow. Finally he will fall flat on the floor realizing that the referee is counting him out of the match and that he can do nothing to prevent it.

The Heart Blow

The heart blow gives a man a sinking sensation. The heavy jar interferes momentarily with the heart action, generally causing him to lower his hands and he falls forward. He will feel the effects of the blow for many hours afterward.

The knockout is a development of modern fighting methods. In the old days the boxers wore a man down by literally pounding him to pieces and after a match opponents often were disabled for days. Contests frequently lasted hours and were unmistakably brutal, a marked contrast to the bouts of today. John L. Sullivan was the first pugilist to demonstrate the possibilities of these blows and since his day they have come into universal use.

FAMOUS BLOWS AND THEIR ORIGINATORS

Fitzsimmon's Contribution

An interesting feature to boxers of the up-to-date school has been the introduction of a number of different blows by certain fighters and with whom they are always associated. First among these is the famous solar plexus punch, which came into prominence in the fight at Carson City, where Robert Fitzsimmons won the world's heavyweight championship from James J. Corbett. This blow had been used before but it was the Cornishman who demonstrated its possibilities by adding a shift, giving terrific force and accuracy. The pit of the stomach, or solar plexus, is well known as a vital part, and when struck, especially if a man is somewhat exhausted, when a slight tap will materially affect him, the distress which follows will oftentimes cause him to collapse.

The M'Coy Corkscrew

The 'corkscrew' blow was evolved by 'Kid' McCoy and as its name would lead one to think, is very deceptive. This punch is delivered to the chin with the left hand and at the moment of impact the arm is straightened out to full length, the hand bring turned palm downward. In delivering this blow you must be at short range. Take the fighting position with the left hand ready to lead as usual, being careful to have the hand tightly clenched, with the palm turned upward. Step in, driving the hand over or under his guard and turning the palm downward with a sudden snap just as the blow lands. A well-developed tricep and swiftness of execution make the blow effective. As the fist lands it is from 3 to 5 inches higher or lower than the line of its original course, according to the height of the opponent. A dropping forward of the shoulder adding its full power contributes to the blow's effect.

The Kidney Punch

The kidney punch, made famous by George Dawson, instructor at the Chicago Athletic Club, is a short, chopping blow, which may be varied by ducking a left lead to the face and swinging your right to the left kidney, and vice versa. This blow is very painful, frequently dangerously injurious, and should not be used by non-professionals. All knockout punches, in fact should be barred from the amateur's repertoire.

The Liver Punch

A blow that I have developed and introduced on various occasions is the liver punch. I always deliver it with my left hand. After feinting my opponent into a lead with his right, which leaves his body exposed, I step in and land a short, stiff uppercut over the liver as he inclines forward. This blow is not particularly dangerous but it readily puts a man out of commission.

At frequent intervals boxers put on the market for public delectation punches which they claim to have discovered and which they state will do nothing short of revolutionizing the science. These products usually go to add zest to the 'silly season', for few have any real claim to merit, and are generally too complicated to be of practical use. But then it gives the press agents opportunities to get to work and the followers of Fistiana a new topic for discussion.

The Science of Boxing

A few hints on the general tactics to be observed while sparring will not go amiss, I trust, before delving into the details and technicalities of the boxing science. The average man and youth that first takes up the study of the great pastime seems to have an idea that he must rush right in at his opponent, with his head down and his eyes shut, swinging his arms wildly as if fighting a swarm of bees. Of course it is all right to be enthusiastic, but never let anything take the place of cool calculation. In fact boxing, above all other sports, requires that the actions of its followers be governed by generalship and judgment. Generalship is even more important in the ring than in a football or baseball game. The boxer should be like a winning jockey who uses caution during the early part of a race and then as the opportunity arises, takes advantage of it in a second's time. When your long-sought-for opening has been found, take for your keynote the words of a famous literary man who once wrote, 'Do not delay; do not delay;

the golden moments fly.' That is sound advice which every boxer can follow with certain reward. It is always a good plan to 'try out' your opponent before getting under full headway. In this manner you will learn his style and ability, his speed, his reach, his strong points and his weak ones. Notice just what particular modes of attack puzzle him and that find him unprepared to guard; learn if possible the blows in which he places the most dependence and also endeavor to ascertain as to whether he is of a nervous temperament, one that may be easily worried. When you have fathomed these points to the best of your ability, you will be all the better prepared to follow an effective line of action. In sizing up a man in this way it is advisable to work to your right, that is, in outside of his left, thus keeping out of direct range of his right, with which hand the most dangerous blows are usually landed. This manoeuvre has been followed by many prominent fighters with good results.

And another point I want to call to the attention of beginners, as well as the more experienced boxers, is that no man should expect to indulge in sparring unless he is prepared to receive punishment from his opponent. Extreme roughness among amateurs is, of course, to be avoided, but every glove manipulator, no matter how expert he may be, is sure to get some hard blows once in a while, and the more unconcernedly he takes them, the better he will get along. Some boxers there are that lose all their presence of mind when they begin to get the worst of a bout. When a couple of heavy punches take effect on them they charge recklessly across the floor like a Kansas cyclone. That will never do. Learn to grit your teeth and keep 'everlastingly at it', as the old time expression goes, and by all means, even if you do get 'rattled', do not let your antagonist become aware of it.

It may sound strange to some people, but it is nevertheless true that punishment helps to make boxing the splendid sport that it is. A man learns to restrain himself under trying circumstances and consequently his self possession in other walks of life becomes stronger also. This restraint enables him to better keep his temper in check, and besides he will obtain a physical hardihood which will always stand him in good stead.

Sparring For An Opening

After having your gloves well adjusted, step in briskly to meet your opponent. Give him a friendly handshake and take your position for action. On beginning the bout, it is always advisable to spar for an opening for in this way, and as I have before stated, you will be able in a measure to judge his tactics. Feinting and footwork will best 'draw him out'. In a very few moments the contest will be on in full swing and you must bring your resourcefulness, instinct and muscle into play. And right here I want to impress on the mind of very boxer the value and even the necessity of hard thinking throughout every bout. Make your brain a most important adjunct to your sparring apparatus, remembering that keen insight and good judgment have won many a victory and have saved scores of men from ignominious defeat. The man that is quick witted can often turn into a triumph what seems to be a forlorn hope. Never close your eyes while sparring for an opening or in any other part of a match. This is a fault common with many amateurs and gives an alert opponent a fine chance to do damage. At the close of the bout do not neglect to again shake hands with your opponent to dismiss any unfriendly feeling which may have arisen during the heat of a moment.

The Straight Left-hand Blow to the Face

In executing the fundamental boxing blow – the straight left-hand punch to the face – great care should be taken to extend the arm to its full length, thus getting the entire benefit of your reach. A man's reach, if it be long, is a decided advantage and no one should fail to derive from it the fullest possible benefit. If a man's reach is short, he can partially overcome it by dropping the shoulder forward as he strikes, adding from 2 to 3 inches to the extension. The straightening of the arm, simultaneously with a step in, also gives more snap and force to the punch.

Do not fail to turn the head to the right, dropping the chin, while delivering this blow.

The chin should always be kept well down while boxing. This position protects the throat and lessens the bad effects of many blows to the head. The straight left to the face is one of the four blows of which all others are variations to a greater or lesser degree. The remaining three are the straight left to the body, the straight right to the face, and the right to the body.

The Straight Right-hand Lead to the Face or Body

A straight right hand lead to the face or body is very hard to evade when delivered accurately. In regard to straightening the arm the same precautions should be observed as in leading with the left. This blow, when sent to the heart, is often used in following up a straight left to the face. Peter Jackson used it in practically all of his big battles. By sending the blow to the body you can attain greater accuracy than by sending it to the head, for you thus have a larger space on which to land and a shorter distance to send the fist.

The Left-hand Jab to the Face

Another hard blow to evade is the left hand jab to the face, because it is delivered at very close range. It is not particularly dangerous, but it is always more or less disconcerting.

A left-hand jab to the face is a snappy blow. The elbow is bent before delivery and the hand points at your opponent's chin. It gets its force from the sudden straightening of the arm as you step in. If you have a strong and aggressive man before you it is well to resort to jabbing until you get him into a position where you can land a heavy blow. Footwork should have its play in jabbing, for oftentimes you will be forced to retreat before the sought for opening presents itself.

Jabbing always plays a prominent part in distance gauging. The left-hand jab to the face is usually followed up with the right to the jaw or body, especially if you have forced your opponent's head well back. In guarding this blow, hold yourself well back, inclining from the waist, throw your right hand across your face, receiving the attacking fist in the palm, which has been opened, and turned outward. In this way you will force his blow wide, many times leaving you an opening for the body or face.

The left-hand jab to the body is not very frequently used simply because there is not enough force in it to materially retard your opponent's advance, unless you can reach the pit of his stomach. In that necessarily delicate spot, even a light blow will make itself felt.

*The Left-hand Lead to the Face and Counter to
the Body*
In countering a left-hand lead to the face, raise
your right forearm across the face so as to block
your opponent's hand by receiving the blow on
the wrist or forearm. At the same time step in,
shooting the left straight to the body, which
blow is also blocked by your opponent's right
if he is watchful. Then spring back quickly into
a defensive position.

Slipping a Left Lead for the Head (A Double Slip)
The slip is often brought into play when you
can feint your opponent into leading for your
head so that you can counter with your left. By
slipping his lead and the intended blow going
over your shculder, he will lunge toward you
into your counter, which you send straight to
the head. He in turn will slip your counter, if he
is on the lookout, and you may fall into a trap
similar to the one you yourself set. Consequently,
do not relax your vigilance. Unless you spring
back quickly you are likely to be hit in the body
with his right. The double slip is spectacular,
and aside from its utility, it contributes greatly
to the attractiveness of a bout. A man must be a
good judge of distance, speed and time in order
to slip properly and effectively.

Blocking a Left-hand Lead to the Body and Countering with a Left Hook to the Face

A straight left hand to the body is best met by the opened palm of the right hand. As the blow comes toward you, place your guard in position, turning your body slightly to the left and forward; step in, countering instantly to your opponent's face with a left-hand hook. By turning your body in the fore going manner you present a smaller target for the attacking blow and increase the length of your reach, which gives the counter dangerous force. If your antagonist is wary he will block your counter by bringing up his right, stopping your fist in his opened palm or shoving it outside. By drawing his chin down behind his right hand he will guard himself perfectly from the hook.

At the conclusion of this blow and counter the man receiving the original lead will be in the better position to make the next lead, his left hand naturally being near his opponent's face and his right drawn back close to his stomach, from whence he can send it over to the face or the body as his combatant draws back. If the opponent springs quickly back, however, he will avoid both the right and the left. This exchange of punches is of frequent occurrence in boxing, and every glove manipulator should take care that he understands clearly the details of the lead, the guard, the counter and the recovery involved.

*Crouching and Sending the Left Straight
to the Body*

By working in a crouch when leading with the left a terrific blow can be sent to the body. And the beauty of this blow consists in its being absolutely safe for the attacker when properly delivered.

To land this blow you must feint your opponent into a lead with his left, and as he does so, step in and crouch, turning your head and body to the right, driving your left straight from the shoulder, using the full force of the shoulder and back muscles and the momentum of the body. Be sure to keep the head well down to the right behind the left shoulder, exposing to your opponent nothing more than the back of your head. Place the right hand over the pit of the stomach ready for action. If your left lead takes the desired effect follow it up immediately with your right hand, which you can send either to the body or to the head with sure knockout impetus. To land the right on the body, turn, facing your opponent squarely by pivoting on the ball of your right foot. Do not straighten more than half out of the crouch or else you will sacrifice a great deal of your power. In sending the right to the face straighten up with arm as it goes over, making one continuous move of the whole blow. By striking on either side of the chin a knockout is certain to result. In delivering either one of these right-hand blows, draws the left back, throwing the forearm across your face with the palm outward, taking an effectual guard.

The left-arm guard and crouch was used most successfully in the memorable fight at Coney Island, New York, where James Jeffries met and defeated Robert Fitzsimmons in their first battle. Jeffries worked this crouch throughout the greater part of the fight, holding off the Cornishman with the left hand.

The following up of a crouching left lead to the body with the right is the most formidable punch in which the right hand figures. In no other blow do so many agencies combine to give that desirable quantity-force. The use of the crouch in its various forms has added considerably to the success of various fighters, and, aside from Jeffries, Terry McGovern and Youni, Corbett found it to have certain advantages. McGovern will oftentimes combine the crouch with a rush, using his hands and arms in piston-rod fashion, literally carrying opponents off their feet. The position in itself is a protection to the body.

The Right-hand Cross-counter For the Head

The right-hand cross-counter for the head is used when you have drawn your opponent into leading a straight left to the face by feinting with your left and leaving an apparent opening to lure him on. Judge your distance carefully, and if too far away to reach him step in driving your right across his left upper arm

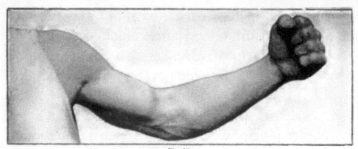

Fig. 16.

PROPER POSITION OF HAND AND ARM FOR LEFT HOOK TO FACE.

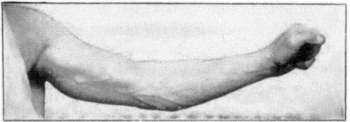

Fig. 17.

IMPROPER POSITION OF HAND AND ARM FOR LEFT HOOK.

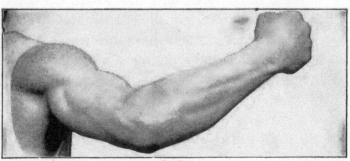

Fig. 18.

PROPER METHOD OF HOLDING RIGHT ARM AND HAND FOR RIGHT HOOK TO THE FACE.

Fig. 19.

IMPROPER WAY OF HOLDING ARM AND HAND FOR RIGHT HOOK TO THE FACE.

and shoulder, at the same time inclining your body and turning your head well to the left. Your fist will strike your combatant on the left side of the chin, completing a well-known knockout. Your punch is given additional force by the momentum of your opponent's body as he comes toward you it leading with his left.

As in all other blows, you should bear in mind the position of the hand your opponent has held in reserve. While taking care of his left in the right cress do not neglect to reach out with your left to his right or guarding hand, checking a possible lead.

In case your fellow boxer does not show shiftiness in getting away from the right-hand cross you can draw your hand back to a striking position and send a short arm punch to the body, stepping in with the left foot the blow is sent over. The heart is easily within reach of this bst blow and its force can be made such as to lay him open to further attack with either hand.

Slipping a Right-hand Cross-counter to the Head
When you have sent a forcible straight left hand to your combatant's face, a right-hand cross-counter which he attempts to deliver may be avoided in three ways: First, by slipping; second, by forcing his arm aside, and, third, by jumping back out of reach. The counter is best slipped when you find that you have wrongly gauged your opponent's ability in this branch of boxing and have placed

yourself at a disadvantage by inclining forward too much with your punch. Quick as a lightning flash you duck your head, throwing it smartly to the right. His fist will then glide harmlessly over the back of your head or neck. To force the blow aside make a short attempt at a lead with the left hand, to draw his right-hand cross, and as it comes toward you throw the left arm up, turning the palm of the hand outward, your forearm striking his forearm on the inside, throwing it outward and wide of the mark.

In springing out of distance of a right cross, feint at your opponent's face with your left hand, causing him to expect a straight lead with it, and when you have decoyed him into sending his right hand over, step back handily with the right foot, inclining the body backward and allowing the blow to fall short. This frequently draws him off his balance. By so doing you bring yourself into position to return your left to any exposed point. There are occasional times when your opponent's right cross will resemble a swing and in these instances all you have to do is to duck swiftly, bending at the knees and waist and inclining the head.

Slipping a Straight Right Lead for the Face and Countering with a Left Swing to the Body
The extreme force usually behind right-hand blows makes it particularly necessary for them to be avoided and, of course, in such a manner that a return is possible. By slipping a right lead

sent straight to the face, a splendid opportunity is had to counter with a strong blow, a left swing, to a part of the body difficult for your opponent to guard.

As your adversary sends his hand over, draw back your left, quickly straightening it out to the left, and, simultaneous with the inclination of the head, to periect the slip, bring the left arm forward to his body with all the force you can muster, but with not so much as to throw yourself off your balance. It is best to send your fist to your opponent's short ribs, for that part of his anatomy will be difficult for him to cover with his guarding hand, which, through the nature of his original load, must be the left. If he is on the alert however, he will be able to throw his left across his body and receive your counter on the back of his glove.

In countering the right-hand lead with your left, hold your right in readiness to deliver a strong blow to either your opponent's face or body. He will naturally incline to the tight. Somewhat after leading, and your right, if well timed and accurately directed, should ferret out an unprotected spot.

Drawing away from Right Swing to Counter with Straight Hand to Face
When your opponent attempts a right swing to your face it is not necessary that the blow be blocked or shoved aside. It can be avoided in a

much easier way, and one which will leave you in a fine position to send in a telling return. As the swing comes toward you, bend back quickly from the waist, still keeping the head erect, thus allowing the swing to fall short and pass harmlessly by. Your left hand and arm should guard your body and your left should be held about opposite the right nipple, so that the return can be sent in swiftly. As your opponent's hand passes your face, shoot your right straight over his swinging arm to his face. Much weight can be put into the blow, and its suddenness, moreover, is decidedly disconcerting to the receiver.

Watch closely your opponent's left as you deliver the blow. He will probably have it drawn back for an opening, and if you expose yourself needlessly you will probably have reason to regret your carelessness. The careless boxer is never a success. While he may show brilliancy at intermittent Intervals, he usually comes out of the small end of the horn in the long run. Get back as quickly as possible from delivering the punch, for if you lean forward any length of time you place yourself at close quarters with the advantage of position all on the other.

RELATING TO HOOKS

Proper Position of Hand and Arm for
Left Hook to Face

Hooks are blows of such frequent ill usage and of such unmistakable value that every boxer should learn to adapt them to his repertory as well to avoid them when directed at him. The hook is a quick blow and is well described by its name, being delivered with a half-bent arm. Hooks are generally sent to the face and, of course, are delivered at close range. They serve admirably to work an opponent into a position where a finishing blow may be delivered.

Great care should be observed in regard to the proper position of the arm and the correct clinching of the fist while hooking. The hook is a forceful punch, and should these points be neglected the results lo tlie boxer will be very unpleasant, broken bones in the hand or arm probably resulting.

To deliver a hook, say with the left, bend the arm so that the hand will be raised around 5 inches above the line of the elbow. The palm should be turned upward and inclined from the wrist somewhat toward the breast, the knuckles compact and if possible in perfect alignment, the thumb being held well down below the line of the middle joints of the finers, as I have instructed in an earlier chapter.

Improper Position of Arm and Hand for Left Hook
The faults in executing a left hook to the face
are mainly to be seen when the combatants have
been instructed in a slipshod manner. One of the
shining defects is usually in the poise of the arm.
Novices are particularly prone to straighten it
out as though making ready for a swing, and
as a result the blow lacks force and accuracy.
Then again they turn the palm and forearm
downward, losing the effect of the strong
arm muscles which are placed in an awkward
position when the hand is held in this manner.
When a blow is landed from the foregoing
improper position the thumb and knuckle
of the forefinger frequently come in contact
with the opponent and when a hard surface
is struck, the skull for instance, painful injury
is apt to follow. This faulty hook is very easily
blocked or thrust aside. The thumb should not
be stuck out in a straight line, projecting above
the line of the middle joints where a slight blow
will often bring disaster.

*Proper Method of Holding Arm and Hand for
Right Hook to the Face*
The right hook to the face is used less frequently
than the left-hand blow, but it is more effective
once it gets through an opponent's guard.
The position of the arm and hand should
correspond to that of the left under the same
circumstances, the only difference in the two

hooks is that they come from opposite sides of the body.

In this hook, as in others, be careful about your feet. They can be made a valuable adjunct to a hook if the boxer knows his business. At the moment the punch lands, your right heel should be raised from the floor, the toes touching it so that you can pivot in either direction. Rising on your toes at times also increases the length of the reach. The leverage of the shoulder should be put into this punch and the back muscles also can be called into play with advantage. Turn the body slightly to the kit as the fist hits the mark, which action will put added weight in the punch.

Improper Method of Holding Hand and Arm For Right Hook To The Face

The faults in an uneducated right hook arc identical with those seen in the beginner's left hook. For the right hand and arm I recommend the same rules I gave for the left. Always brace the arm strongly as the punch takes effect, making the forearm, upper arm, shoulder and back work in with each other. Of course, you will use your free arm to guard, and a sharp lookout must be kept for returns. Do not lead while standing flat on your feet. A step in and a rise to the toes of the right foot are absolutely necessary for the success of every hook.

In hooking to the face do not drop the arm too low before sending the blow over. By dropping the fist very low the punch is longer in taking effect and the time lost gives your opponent ample opportunity to block it. Do not let your hooks resemble uppercuts too closely; neither copy the swinging style unless you really intend to swing. Hooks to the face may be landed behind either ear, on either side of the chin, or either eye.

Shifting From Straight Left Lead to Head and Countering with Right to Body

When your opponent shoots a straight left directly at your face you must think and act very rapidly. Indeed, quickness of thought and action are the foundation of all boxing success. One good way of a voiding this lead is to shift suddenly to the left, stepping in forward and to the left around 6 inches, allowing the lead to glide over your right shoulder. Counter this blow by sending in a stiff right-hand jab to your opponent's body, putting into it the impetus of the body as you step in. His body will naturally come toward you as he delivers his punch and this, too, will make your blow the more powerful. The short ribs or the heart can be reached with equal ease, as the straight left will leave the left side wide open. During the course of the foregoing blow and counter you must guard your face and body with your left arm, which you will double in front of you. The right of your adversary has not yet been brought into action and he will probably have it drawn back close to his body for instant use. You will be going toward him and should you chance to meet this right with an unprotected spot the contact will not be to your advantage.

Shoving Aside Opponent's Left Lead with Your Right and Countering to Body with Left
Another manner of avoiding and countering a straight left to the head is as follows:
Meet the blow with the palm of your right glove, forcing your opponent's fist to one side, over the left shoulder. Hold your own body erect, with the exception of your head, which should be inclined forward somewhat, and step in, sending your feft across to his body, preferably to the solar plexus.

If your opponent knows what to do and when to do it, he will meet your counter with his right, which is supposed to have been reserved for this very purpose. You can sometimes follow your left with your right if you choose by bringing it down from its position in shoving aside the left lead and delivering it to your combatant's body. But you must be very quick if you wish to do this or he will get away from you.

Keep your eyes pinned on your fellow boxer throughout the entire process; in fact never turn them entirely away from him during any part of a bout, and, if possible, pin his right hand – if it has blocked your left counter –

firmly to his body with your band until you have a chance to spring out of striking distance.

Stopping a Right-hand Cross-counter to Head with Left to Follow with Inside Left Hook to Jaw

After a series of feints with your left you will probably draw your opponent into leading a right cross-counter to your jaw, he naturally supposing that you intended to send in a straight left with each feint. You intended to deceive him and expected him to act in this manner. When you see his cross-counter start, step in and meet it. Strike his right forearm on the inside with your left forearm, holding off the blow. Stop your left arm momentarily gauging the distance to his face, and deliver a short left-hand hook to the jaw, dropping the body forward, inclining the head sharply to the right your combatant's right arm will shoot across the back of your head or neck.

In the meantime your opponent has probably held his left in readiness to follow up his counter to the face or body. On finding that he has missed connection with his left and has been reached by your left, he will, if not in a dazed condition, withdraw from close quarters, discovering that you are well on guard with your right.

These inside short hooks were first brought into prominence by Robert Fitzsimmons. Practically all of his fights in which opponents would mix with him resulted in his favor. Jeffries usually kept from continuing close work with

Fitzsimmons, and during the last battle of these giants at San Francisco the result of Jeffries' close-range tactics is well known to the public. For the first few rounds the long, lean, freckled Cornishman battered the ex-boilermaker unmercifully. Fitzsimmons has introduced several new features into the boxing art, and it was partly through these that he was enabled to pit himself successfully against men stronger and heavier than himself.

Blocking a Left Swing to Body and Delivering a Short Left Swing to Face
The uncertainty of a bout in which feinting plays a prominent part is plainly shown in an exchange of blows I will now describe.

Take the regulation fighting position and send in a series of straight left feints to your opponent's face, keeping your right or guarding arm higher than necessary. This guard will tempt the opponent into leading at the spot he considers neglected.

He does this by stepping outside of your left foot with his left and swing his left hand to the body as he moves forward. You block this swing by bringing down the right hand forcibly, throwing the blow wide by striking it with the forearm or wrist. At the same time you counter with a left swing to the jaw. As you expected, your opponent was probably unprepared for this swinging blow, thinking that you would lead the usual straight left, and he, intending to slip the punch, receives it fully in the face before he has time to block it with his right or duck. Right here is another case where cardessness resulted disastrously to a boxer. In not having his guarding hand in position to protect the face, particularly that vital spot, the point of the jaw, your combatant laid himself open to your attack, and as your blow that landed was a swing, in many cases he would most certainly have been transferred to the realm of shooting stars, about which we hear so much in connection with boxing. And it is highly probable that h e would not have been able to discontinue his astronomical researches until after knockout count of ten seconds, or possibly twenty or thirty.

Slipping a Straight Left Lead to Head and
Delivering a Left-hand Uppercut to Body
In sparring for an opening and your opponent seems unusually wary of you and you do not appear to be able to draw him out, it is sometimes advisable to place in his way some tempting bait. This can be done by leaving your head unguarded. It is noticeable that a majority of blows, especially those of amateurs, are usually led to the head and whenever an opening for it is presented, the natural inclination is to take advantage of it, hence the value of throwing out a lure. When the bait has the desired effect,

drawing him into the handiest blow for him to land a straight left lead for the face, it can be disposed of and blocked in several ways. One of the most effective proceedings is to slip it by stepping in with the left foot, inclining the head and body to the right, and delivering a short left-hand uppercut to the pit of the stomach.

Should this blow take full effect it will greatly distress your opponent, probably causing him to collapse. If however, he is on his guard, with his right in proper protecting position, he can meet the uppercut with the palm of the opened glove, as shown in the illustration, forcing it downward.

The uppercut calls to play a combination of muscular effort that gives it vast power and the guard for it should not be such as may easily be driven back. The upward movement of the arm is assisted by the straightening of the right leg and by rising to the ball of the right foot. This uppercut may be avoided in part, if not wholly, by drawing back the body from the waist, and which action will straighten the legs.

The Corkscrew Blow

Among the so-called 'fancy blows' but one, the solar plexus is more widely known than the 'corkscrew' punch, the invention of that brilliant Hoosier boxer, Kid McCoy. As I have previously described the nature of this punch I will now tell you how to secure a chance for landing it and also how it may be avoided when used by an opponent.

The corkscrew is most effectively delivered when your opponent has taken the aggressive. Keep him in striking distance of the extended left arm and as you induce him into leading with either hand, preferably the right, step in, if you find it necessary, and 'corkscrew' your left to his face in the manner described under the heading 'Famous Blows'.

To best guard against the corkscrew crouch quickly, holding your right arm well in front of your chin, letting the attacking hand go wide and over the left shoulder. In this position you will find yourself ready to step in and send your left hand straight to the face or body. Should your opponent be well on his guard I advise you to retreat by stepping back. Should the corkscrew land, finding you unguarded, and does not jar you too heavily, you can follow it up with a left hook to the face or body, keeping your right hand well in front of your face.

Ducking a Left Swing and Countering to Body with a Left Swing

When your opponent appears to be tiring or shows effects of overtraining he will generally start in to swing, especially if inexperienced, thinking to turn the tide his way with a single blow. You should not discourage him in this tendency, but rather endeavour to lead him on. Of course, these wild attempts leave a man wide open to attack, and while in a measure his blows are to be feared, they may be avoided in various ways. Above all keep cool under these circumstances and let him 'fight himself out' by exhausting his strength and wind.

When your opponent arrives at the swinging stage, through over-anxiety or lack of proper instruction, do not be too anxious to place him *hors de combat*, but measure his reach and speed, moving about him carefully, the while trying to feint him into a right-hand swing so that you can send your right to the left short ribs. But on the contrary, if he disappoints you by swinging the left. Duck your head smartly to the right, step forward, outside of his left foot, and swing your left behind forcibly to his stomach. He can block your return, if he is careful, by placing his right hand across the body before swinging.

If your fellow boxer over-reaches himself on missing the swing, pitching forward off his balance and floundering helplessly, you can immediately straighten up and deliver either hand to the most favorable opening.

*Slipping a Straight Left Lead for Face and
Delivering a Right-hand Blow to the Body*
By the slipping of a straight left for the face in the proper manner you will place yourself in a

splendid position to brin your right into effective use. As your antagonist strikes at you with his left hand, step slightly forward and to your left, slipping the blow, allowing it to pass over your right shoulder. Your opponent will naturally lunge forward as his hand misses the mark and you should then jolt him heavily with a half-arm right-hand blow to the body, permitting the trunk of your body to swing around to the left with the punch, putting added force behind it.

Be careful about the position of your head in executing this manoeuvre, keeping it inclined forward, close to your opponent's chest, so that be cannot easily reach it. Should your right-hand blow be blocked with your opponent's right, which he will do if be is on the alert, step in with your left foot and hook your left hand swiftly in his face. Follow up your attack as opportunity offers.

The right-hand body blow, after the slipping of a left lead, is a particularly good punch to be perfected by men capable of delivering a strong half-arm right to the body. Many men are so put together physically that their punches vary in force according to the elevation of the point at which they strike. Take a stocky, thick-set man for instance, of the George 'Kid' Lavigne type. He will be at his best when sending in body blows, because his principal hitting muscles are set low, giving the greatest power to punches in which these muscles are brought fully into play.

The rangey man of the Fitzsimmons stamp, whose hitting power lies chiefly in his high shoulder muscles, is at his best in delivering punches to the head.

In sparring with a man that depends a great deal on the short right body punches, make a snappy feint at his face with your left hand, getting him to step in and attempt to lead with his right. Before he can recover himself, step in and send a swift straight left jab to his face.

Pinning Your Opponents Right with Your Left and Delivering a Right Hook to the Jaw

When your opponent draws his hand well back to deliver a short hook or swing to the jaw, step in to close quarters, reaching out with your left hand and laying your opened hand over his right wrist with enough resistance to check any move he intends. This constitutes a left-hand pin. At the same time lead a short straight right hook to his jaw, inclining the body forward and to the left. By keeping close to your opponent you will rob him of the force of his left in case he should attempt to lead a short blow to your body. Your head will be entirely ont of danger.

The effectiveness of this blow depends largely on the manipulation of the legs and feet. The diagonal step to the left should occur as the blow starts underway and, of course, is done with the left foot. Just as the blow lands, rise

well on the toes of the right foot, straightening
the left leg. This will elevate your right shoulder,
giving you a longer reach and increased force
to the blow.

When this punch is sent in properly you need
have no fear of your combatant's left. Should
you miss, by your opponent drawing away
from the hook or ducking, you will naturally
fall into close quarters. Then you should clinch
and save yourself.

The Utility of Clinching
And now that I have mentioned the subject of
clinching I will briefly explain the value of the
service to which it may be put. In case you lead
a blow that falls short or is evaded in any way,
and by so doing you have left yourself at close
range open to attack, it is best to throw your
arms around those of your opponent, pinning
his elbows with your forearm and holding
them close to his body by locking your hands
behind him. Then straighten up to him as close
as possible, and as you break away draw your
hands gradually along his arms, pressing them
firmly until the moment when you can spring
liack into a fighting attitude.

I do not advise frequent clinching, as it makes
a bout long and tiresome and detracts from its
interest as a scientific exhibition. Unless you
are entirely out of wind, depend rather on

footwork and deft guarding to help you in case of emergency.

The Liver Punch

The liver punch is one of frequent use and when delivered with considerable force is extremely painful. A first-class opportunity to send in this blow is offered when your opponent swings with his right. This leaves the right side of his body more or less exposed. To counter a right swing with this punch, step inside of your opponent's arm as it comes toward you and shoot your left into his body directly over the liver, which is situated on the right side slightly below the floating ribs.

Hold your right hand in front of your chest and close to your body with the palm opened and turned toward your antagonist in most instances. In this manner you will be prepared to block or ward off his left, which he has probably been holding in reserve to follow up his right swing. As you step in to avoid the swing, incline your head forward so that the attacking hand will strike the back of the head or neck.

The punch I have described has been used on many occasions with good effect by Kid McCoy. Of course it takes courage to step inside of a swing and you must be accurate in timing your opponent's delivery and in gauging his distance. After a little practice you will find yourself becoming absolutely fearless in stepping in and you will be surprised at the degree of efficiency to which you can attain in performing the manoeuvre.

Ducking a Right-hand Swing and Getting in a Position to Send Either Hand to Body

Having described the manner in which to stay inside of a righthand swing for the head, I will now tell you how to avoid it in another way – by ducking. As you see the swing coming toward you, duck quickly so that the attacking hand will pass over your head, at the same time keeping both hands extended somewhat before your chest, so that you will be able to use either one in countering the attacker's body. He will probably have his left drawn across his stomach to guard a return, and in that case endeavor to reach his face. This do by lunging forward as you duck the swing, and, pinning his guard with either hand, send the free hand to the jaw. Probably the best hand to use in hitting will be the right, consequently the hand to do the pinning will be the left.

Do not be too anxious to attack immediately after ducking the swing, however. A little caution will often do more good than an attempt to strike. If your opponent has held himself well in control after missing the swing he may be prepared for you, no matter what you lead, and in that case the best thing for you, to do is to spring back into position.

Blocking an Opponent's High Left Swing for the Head and Standing Ready to Block His Right Jab to the Body

Oftentimes an opponent will charge strongly at you, intending to attack with both hands. A good combination of blows, which is frequently used is the right left swing for the held, followed up by a forceful right jab to the body. To effectually protect yourself, meet his swing by throwing out your right arm, allowing his attacking wrist to strike your forearm and as he sends the right across at your body, block it with the opened palm of your left, meeting the fist about midway between you. His head and shoulders will be inclined somewhat toward you, and if you are quick you can bend your right hand downward to his face from the point of contact with his swing. By standing erect, with the head pitched forward a trifle, you will not suffer any evil consequences and will better be able to obtain a commanding view of the situation and judge as to your best move.

Stepping Outside to the Right of a Straight Left to Head and Delivering Left Swing to Head

If you have a good eye and are very quick, you can avoid a straight left lead for the head by stepping outside of it. A straight left lead is one of the hardest blows to evade in this manner and to do it successfully it is absolutely necessary that a man be extremely agile.

The shorter the distance of your opponent's lead, the quicker you must be in getting out of the way. You must incline your head sharply in the direction you go, also turning your head away from the punch, but not so far as to place your opponent out of the range of vision.

A very forcible blow which you may deliver as you step outside is a left swing to the face. Your left shoulder is thrown upward as you incline to the right, thus giving a better opportunity to land the swing strongly and accurately. In stepping out to the right for instance, carry your left foot up and over your opponent's left toes, placing your foot almost opposite his heel, which will put you close enough to him to prevent your swinging past him. As you step in in this manner, allowing his left lead to go over your left shoulder, swing your left hand downward and to the rear, contracting firmly the muscles of the arm and turning your clenched fist palm downward. As you bring it forward, turn the fist so that the face of the knuckles will come in contact with your fellow boxer as the blow lands. The blow should start as the left foot touches the floor beyond your opponent's left and as it takes effect you should be braced firmly on both feet in order to bring your entire power into it.

Should the punch be blocked by your opponent's right, bring your left back in a direct line with your left shoulder, inclining titill more to the right and swing again, sending the fist to the pit of the stomach. Let your body come around with the blow, and it will have telling effect.

After delivering the swing to the head you can oftentimes deceive your opponent by stepping out and feinting the swing, but instead of delivering it, let your hand go as close to his face as possible without hitting him and bring it back with the quickest you are capable of, sending it to his body before he can get his right hand down to guard. Under all circumstances you are too far to the right to be reached by either hand before you can safely retreat.

Stepping to the Right of a Straight Left to Heart and Countering with a Short Left Swing to Heart
After drawing your opponent into a straight left lead to your heart, step outside to the right in the manner I have already described and deliver a half arm swing with your left under his attacking arm to the solar plexus. You will have to crouch considerably to escape the lead and as you deliver your left straighten up, rising well on the toes of your right foot, then spring backward to your right into fighting position.

Stepping Inside of a Left Swing to Head and
Delivering a Half-arm Right-hand Blow to Body

While sparring and you notice that your
opponent is anxious to swing at your head, lead
him on by inclining toward him, causing him
to think you are closer than you really are, and
expose your head. As he swings for it, say with
his left, step in and incline to the left allowing
his swinging forearm to strike the back of your
neck. At the same time contract your right arm
firmly, sending a jolt to the heart. Pin his right
with your left, and you will be perfectly safe from
further attack. You may have an opportunity to
repeat your right to the body unless he clinches
or retreats very quickly.

Avoiding a Straight Right to Face by Stepping to
the Right and Sending Over a Right Chop to Face

I do not particularly advise a man to indulge too
frequently in the chopping habit, but there is
one instance in which this sort of a blow may be
used to advantage, and it requires the bringing
of the right hand into play. I would never use
the chop under any other circumstances unless
it be during a clinch in what is known as 'one
arm free fighting'. A chop can then be used, to
advantage on the kidneys.

The chop which I countenance is delivered
with the right hand after you have evaded a
straight right to the face, allowing it to pass over
your right shoulder. As your opponent's blow

comes toward you, bend to the left, throwing your right arm well up, then send it forward and downward to your opponent's face with the palm turned downward. Hold your left close to your body so that you can follow up your chop by drawing the right hand to guard, and, stepping in, deliver your left to any exposed part of your combatant's body.

The right-hand chop is usually an extremely hard blow to block, especially for beginners, because they are but little accustomed to covering themselves with their left arm as they deliver their right hand. As I have previously explained, no one in boxing should attempt to lead the right without throwing their left arm well over the face and drawing the stomach in out of reach.

The Solar Plexus Punch

I touched briefly on the blow made famous by Robert Fitzsimmons, the solar plexus punch, in the opening part of this book under the title of 'Famous Blows', and I will go into the details of it, telling you how to work your opponent into a position making it possible, and how best to make it thoroughly effective.

Spar around your fellow boxer for a few moments and feint sharply at him several times, bringing both your hands into action. This will usually make him a bit nervous and he will begin to shift his guard to cover the different points you are feinting at. Suddenly Jean forward a trill and feint furiously at your combatant's face wih your right fist. He will naturally bend back to avoid the supposed attack and will throw his guard up to protect his face, leaving the pit of the stomach partially unprotected at least, for in the excitement of the moment the covering of his face will be his principal thought. In the illustration, the opponent has thrown up his right hand in front of his face, holding his left too far to the left to fully protect the objective point. You now have him 'wide open' for the delivery of the punch with your left, which you draw back into a striking position as you feint with the right.

How to Deliver the Solar Plexus

In sending the solar plexus punch home, after you have feinted your man into the desired opening, step in with all the speed and force at your command, and shoot your left heavily into the pit of his stomach, inclining smartly to the right as you do so, rising to the toes of your left foot which rests between his feet close to his left, and bearing the greater part of your weight on your right foot as the punch takes effect. By inclining your body as I have instructed, you will better escape your opponent's left, should he happen to use it, and you will be in a good position to come back at him with your right, which you hold in front of your body as a guard. Of course, the solar plexus punch in its most violent form is to be delivered only in the professional ring and amateurs should take great care in their use of it.

Drawing Back on Guard from a Straight Left to Face and in Position to Send Either Hand to Face or Body

I will now describe a manoeuvre which all boxers can use to advantage and of which ex-champion Corbett has availed himself successfully on various occasions. It is a move calculated to deceive your combatant in gauging you distance, and is performed as follows:

On an occasion when your opponent leads straight to your face with his left, thinking that he has you within range, bend back swiftly from the waist, allowing his fist to fall short several inches, the while keeping your hands in front of your body, your right being just below your chin to meet the attacking hand should your opponent Junge forward as you bend back. Then by inclining slightly to the left and forward you can shoot into his body or face either hand as the occasion warrants. The bend forward from your somewhat strained position in evading the lead will give additional momentum to your attack. Be careful to keep vigilant watch on your antagonist's right, which he probably has drawn back in reserve. Guard your face with either hand as you lunge forward to strike or else you may meet his right unprotected.

Relaiting to Uppercuts

In delivering an uppercut, the final things to be considered ater the proper clenching of the fist, are the poise of the hand and arm. The hand should incline a trifle toward the shoulder by bending at the wrist, and the arm should be extended about two-thirds of its entire length, bending at the elbow. The uppercut is usually sent to the chin and should strike with the face of the knuckles. Considerable leverage can be put into a blow of this sort by making the shoulder muscles figured prominently in it.

Correct Delivery of a Right Uppercut

The right uppercut is sent in with the right arm in a position similar to that of the left under the same circumstances, the muscles of the arm should be well contracted so as to give it the stiffness necessary to make the blow a solid one. Keep the thumb turned well outward. If you turn it inside you place your arm in a position where the full strength of your muscles cannot be utilized. Besides, you thus place your hand in the way of almost certain injury. It is always wise to rise to the ball of foot on the same side as your attacking hand in uppercutting, for thus you will put more weight into it.

*Blocking a Right Swing and Sending a Right
Uppercut to Chin*

When your opponent swings for your head
with his right, you can often block it and
counter very effectively to his chin with a
right uppercut. As he swings, step in and meet
his attacking forearm with your forearm,
which you have bent across your face, and
send quickly to the point of his jaw your
right, starting it from a line just a little below
your waist.

Should your man come back at you with his
left, you can render it void by throwing to meet
it your right, which you will have just used in
uppercutting. Then, quick as a flash, you can
bring down to his face your left, which had to
be raised high to hold off the original swing.
Your body should be traightened up during this
whole operation and you must use your eyes
and your wits as well as your hands and feet.

*Blocking a Left Swing and Sending a Left
Uppercut to Chin*

A swing can be treated in a manner similar to
that in which you disposed of the right in the
foregoing paragraph. Meet the swing with your
right hand or forearm and step in, shooting a
left uppercut to the point of the jaw. As was the
case in using the right, you can easily bring the
guarding hand down to your opponent's face
to follow up your uppercut and in the event

of his returning his right, you can meet it with your left, which you can thrust downward and outward from its point of contact with your antagonist's jaw.

Striking an Opponent's Left Lead on Outside, Forcing His Blow to the Left, Drawing Him Off His Balance and Standing Ready to Send Either Hand to Head or Body

Fitzsimmons frequently resorted to a clever practice which has become of frequent use by different boxers. It consisted in striking or shoving the outside of a man's attacking arm as he led, forcing his fist across the front of his (Fitzsimmon's) body, and far to the side opposite that to which he aimed. By so doing, an opponent is drawn forward off his balance and turned partially around in an awkward and indefensible position. If you are quick you can then use either hand on him with advantageous results.

Should a man lead his left straight to your face yon can execute the aforementioned manoeuvre by grasping his left elbow with the opened palm of your righ hand and shoving it strongly to your left, at the same time inclining slightly to the right. As your opponent swings around you can come forward heavily to his heart with your left or shoot your right to his ribs, head or chop to his left kidney. It is more difficult to handle a right lead in this manner, because is usually carries more force behind it.

*Stepping Outside of a Straight Right Lead,
Pushing it Over Right Shoulder With Left Hand
and Sending Right to Body*

In stepping outside of a straight left to the face you can often force the attacking arm over the right shoulder by shoving the elbow on the outside as it comes toward you. As you do this, step in and send the right to your opponent's body, either the pit of the stomach or the right floating ribs, and spring back quickly into position. A combatant that understands boxing will block your counter by bringing his left in front of his stomach as he sends his right over. If you are snappy in your movements you can withdraw your right in the event of its being blocked and send it up to your fellow boxer's jaw, bringing down your left to guard your body from his left as you do so.

*Blocking a Right Swing to Body with Left and
Standing Ready to Block Left Lead to Face or
Body with Right*

In studying defensive work do not fail to pay close attention to avoiding your opponent when he delivers blows with both hands in rapid succession. Very frequently, especially when a man is rushing you, he will send over one hand and follow it up instantly with the other, thinking to bewilder you, if he does not succeed in making one of his punches take effect.

Often a man will combine a right swing to the body with a left lead for the face, and when he does this brace yourself well Jack and stop his swinging arm with your firmly extended left, holding your right hand 10 or 12 inches in front of your chest with the palm opened to receive the left when it follows. By keeping your right in this position you will find yourself prepared to block either a lead for the body or head by simply lowering or raising it. Brace yourself strongly on your right leg as the blows come over so that the shock you may receive will not throw you off your balance.

Stepping Outside of a Straight Right to Face, Shoving it Over Right Shoulder with Left Hand and Standing Ready to Send Right to Face or Body

The straight right hand of an opponent led to the face may be disposed of in a way exactly the reverse of that used in evading the left. As the blow comes toward you step outside of it and forward pushing the outside of the attacking arm at the elbow so that it will glide over your right shoulder. Instantly shoot the right across to your opponent's face or body, preferably the body, for it is much easier of access in this case than the face. Bring your left back to guard your face as you go forward to avoid leaving an opening for your opponent's left. You can also get away from the left by inclining sharply to the left after shoving your combatant's right over your shoulder.

Blocking with Right Hook to Jaw and Countering with Inside Left Hook to Jaw

The jaw is a favorite objective point with almost every boxer, and you can learn to counter blows for it very effectively. When a man sends at your jaw a right hook you can block it by bending your right arm across your face, receiving the blow in the opened palm, then step in and counter to his jaw with a swift left hook inside of the attacking hook. If you vary with this manceuvre the ordinary blocks and counters for leads to the jaw you will be likely to take your opponent unawares, for when executed with swiftness it is very disconcerting.

As for your opponent's left, it will be in a position to land effectively on your body during the foregoing manceuvre unless you are on the lookout. With your right engaged in blocking his right and your left across to his jaw, your ribs and stomach will present him a tempting mark, which he will speedily find unless you hold your stomach well in and get your right down to guard without delay.

Blocking a Left Hook to Jaw with Left and Countering with Inside Right Hook to Jaw

To block a left hook to the jaw and counter with a right inside hook to your opponent's jaw, bend your left arm across your chest, receiving the blow in the opened palm simultaneously with the delivery of your right. This move is the reverse of the one described in the immediately preceding section. Keep your head erect so that you can command a view of the whole situation and decide quickly as to whether or not you had better follow up your counter or spring back into fighting position. Whatever you do, see that your opponent's strong right does not get a chance to land on your body. He will 'tear you wide open' with it if you are not careful.

Pulling Down an Opponent's Guarding Hand to Make an Opening

A device which is sometimes resorted to by speedy boxers to obtain a temporary advantage is the pulling down of an opponent's guard to make an opening. The slow man cannot do it successfully, for his combatant will immediately see what he is up to and protect himself. As the right hand is most frequently the guard, in nine cases out of ten you would best use your left in drawing it down. Spar warily around your antagonist and when you get him with his guard high and his left down on about a level with his waist, step in, grasping strongly the top of his right fist with your left hand and pull it toward you with all your might, at the same time shooting your right over to his jaw or body. Keep yourself covered with your right as you spring back, for if your man is fast with his left he will be able to follow you and do damage unless you are protected.

Ducking Your Head Under Left Chop to Face and Obtaining Position to Send Either Hand to Body
To demonstrate the evils of chopping I will explain how to evade a left chop to the face in a manner that will probably put your opponent's leading hand 'out of commission' and which will leave you in a distinctly advantageous position. As your man straightens out his high left to chop down to your face, step in and incline your head sharply, allowing his fist to strike the hard skull bones instead of the soft flesh of the face. If he puts much force into the blow his hand will suffer injurious effect. Probably one or two of the small bones will break or become disjointed and he will be effectively cured of the habit of chopping down for the face – when you are opposing him at least. The high position of your opponent's left arm in chopping will leave his body open to some extent and then you can send in your right or your left, according to the best chance offered. It will probably be advisable to pin his right with your left and deliver the right.

Drawing away from a Left Swing to Body and Countering with a Left Hook to Jaw
I cannot emphasize too strongly the value of occasionally drawing in your waist to escape body blows and without altering the position

of the feet. The use of these various defensive moves gives you a desirable versatility of style which will mislead almost any boxer. When a left swing is led for the body you can readily evade it by contracting your waist and pitching your shoulders forward. As you do this, counter to your opponent's jaw with a left hook, which will be all the header when backed by the lunge. When your own swings are evaded and counterd in this manner carry your right arm to your face as a fender for the hook.

Stepping Inside of Straight Left to Head and Countering with Straight Right to Jaw

A very pretty mode of escaping and countering a straight left to the face is to step inside of it and send your right straight to your opponent's jaw. As you counter, incline your head forward and pin his right with your extended left.

The Side Step

The great utility of side-stepping was never appreciated to its full extend until Jim Corbett and Kid McCoy developed the art to the highest point yet attained in the annals of the world's boxing. Where is there a man that has seen either or both of these men box who will not agree that their footwork has given them a position unapproached by any other fighters? Of course, it takes continued practice to become an adept in side-stepping. The leg muscles must be springy and flexible to permit rapid movements and if a slow man is unwilling to take the pains to develop readiness of action he must cut out this accompaniment of sparring.

I have already described in the section entitled 'The Elements of Defence' the exact mode of executing a side step, and I will now give a few hints concerning your attitude toward a man proficient in it. A man will generally side-step to his right, that direction being the easiest for him to travel in through the nature of the regulation boxing position, and also because he will thus place himself out of reach of your right and leave himself in a better position to return your lead. Therefore you should endeavor to conduct yourself so that his attempt to evade you will fall short of his intention. This goes as follows:

Holding your right drawn back in readiness for instant service, lead for your opponent with a straight left. As he performs the expected side step to his right – your left – permitting your left hand to glide past his left shoulder, swing your body around toward him and shoot your right straight to either his face or body as best you can, bringing your left back to guard against any blow he may chance to attempt. Unless your man is possessed of tremendously long legs and is phenomenally active you can in most cases land your fist effectively in this way. You can often feint him into a side-step with your left, but if you send a bonafide lead at him do not put enough force in it to carry you off your balance or else you will place yourself completely at the mercy of his right.

The Safety Block

The safety block is the best guard for the human frame known in boxing. It is not used very frequently, not so often as it should be, in fact, and therefore is unfamiliar to many followers of fistiana.

The block in question brings both hands and arms into use, and has been found very valuable by men when in awkward positions, say in a corner, or against the ropes and hard pressed by an opponent. It consists in folding the right forearm across the face, the nose and chin fitting snugly into the crook of the elbow, and holding the left close to and directly across the front of the body, the upper arm covering the heart and left ribs, the forearm and hand with the palm opened and turned in, protecting the pit of the stomach and right ribs. The block can be made still more of a 'safety' by bending this stomach inward as you carry the arms into position.

When your opponent gets you into a tight place and you cannot force him back by an assault, assume quickly the position as described and you can with impunity advance to any part of the floor or ring, as the case may be. His fists cannot reach a vital part, for by watching him closely and shifting either hand or forearm the merest trifle you can block anything he may choose to deliver. George McFadden has used the safety block successfully on various occasions.

Missing Intentionally a Hook to Jaw and
Delivering a Back Hand Blow to Face

To take a man unawares when he least expects to be surprised is the ambition of every manipulator of the gloves and I will now give the details of a sort of 'double-barrelled' blow which has come to my notice and which has been termed the 'lever punch.' Brace yourself staunchly on your feet and send a left swing at your opponent's jaw, which you intentionally miss by about two or three inches. Allow your hand to go past him, say about two feet, and as he lunges toward you, thinking that you have missed a genuine attempt at his jaw, bring your attacking hand back sharply to his face before he will have time to land on you, hitting his jaw a sort of backhand swing.

Naturally the blow coming in that manner will bewilder your combatant and in the momentary confusion you can follow up your left with your right to the body or perhaps the face. However, if he takes punishment well enough to recover in an instant, sending his left to your body, or if he counters to your body with either his left or right as you strike his jaw, you can ward off the attack in either case with the opened palm of the right hand. Hold your head well elevated with the chin drawn in so that you will be able to take in the whole situation at a glance.

The Clinch

The clinch might well be termed 'the boxer's friend', for it always comes to his aid in times of distress. The best mode of clinching, which I have previously described, is admirably portrayed in illustration above, which shows myself about to release my hold on my opponent's arms. Observe closely the manner in which I have drawn my hands along my sparring partner's arms instead of releasing my grasp with a sudden jump from the original clinch bold around the waist, which latter action will invariably throw you open to one or more of those objectionable breakaway punches. The proper pinning of your opponent's arms as you withdraw from the clinch will always give you the 'balance of power' in the breakaway, both from offensive and defensive viewpoints.

How to Block Opponents Left For Face or Body After He Secures Chancery Hold With Right

When a boxer shoots either right or left hand around an opponent's neck and draws his – the opponent's – head toward himself to deliver a blow to either the face or body, he is said to have secured a 'chancery hold', or to have placed his antagonist's head 'in chancery'. A leading dictionary gives a good description of a chancery hold in defining the term as follows: 'A boxing expression used when the head is caught and securely held under the hand or arm of an opponent,' and no less a personage than the eminent littérateur, Dr Oliver Wendell Holmes, referred to this phase of sparring when he wrote, 'When I can perform my mile in eight minutes or a little less, then I feel as if l had Old Time's head in chancery.'

Although history does not relate that the great poet and essayist was especially active in athletic pursuits, the foregoing quotation shows that he had more than a superficial knowledge of one of the manliest arts ever invented for the amusement and physical betterment of mankind.

The obtaining of a chancery hold is rather a dangerous proceeding – and a man should exercise due caution, for in many instances he will leave an opening for severe punishment. When you place your opponent's head in chancery with your right draw your stomach well in, throwing your shoulders forward, and send in your left to either his face or body. When your combatant gets such a hold on you draw your stomach in again and guard with both hands if you cannot readily reach him with either. Hold your right extended somewhat, with the palm opened, protecting your body, and keep the left near your chin. Sometimes you can rid yourself of this hold by ducking your head sharply forward.

Delivering Right to Body From Inside a Chancery Hold by Opponent's Left

Oftentimes an opponent will secure a chancery hold after you have stepped inside a swing. As his hand strikes the back of your neck after you avoid his swing, and he tries to pull you toward himself with it to deliver his right, shoot your right stiffly to his heart. Hold your left with the palm opened as a guard from his right for your face and body.

Ducking a Left Lead, Pinning Opponent's Right to Body With Left Forearm Against Your Head and Sending Right to Body

Infighting is a term applied to boxing when the contestants are so close to each other as to prevent the delivery of straight arm blows. As is the case in chancery operations, both men must be very careful to keep as well guarded as possible in infighting. A quick man can play havoc with a slow opponent in either branch of the game, so learn to think and act rightly on the spur of the moment, letting no opening go unnoticed when you can take advantage of it with a fair degree of safety.

During infighting, when your opponent leads his necessarily short left to your face, you will often be enabled to work a dodge, which I have found to be very effective. As his hand comes to you, duck forward. allowing it to pass over your right shoulder and bringing your left forearm directly across and against your forehead, lunge forward against him, pinning his guarding right to his body with your combined head and forearm and sending your right to his body, say, the pit of the stomach or left ribs. You should be able to carry him off his balance with the force of your onslaught and follow him up with a spirited attack with both hands. If he stands firm however, spring back out of danger instantly.

Ducking a Short Right Swing While Infighting,
Pinning Opponent's Left With Right and
Countering With Left to Body
Short swings for the head are often resorted to in infighting and when your contestant leads at you in such a manner a blow wiih his right, avoid it and counter as follows. Step in and duck snappily under his attacking arm and it will go harmlessly over your head and shoulders. As you crouch, send your right to block his left by pinning it to his body and with the full momentum of your advance drive your left to the pit of his stomach or left ribs. You can carry your left well back before landing, thus putting considerably more force into it than would ordinarily be the case. Should your man be slow in extricating himself from his dangerous position you can rlraw back

your iefr and shoot it into him once or twice again.

Foul Blows Tactics Which All Boxers Should Avoid

There are many blows which come into boxing usage that are classed under the heading 'Foul Blows'. It is the unprincipled practice of various members of the prizering fraternity to land one of these punches at such moments when they believe they can do so without detection on the part of spectators or referee, or if detected, they think the plea 'accident' will exonerate them from blame. Of course, the fair-minded boxer will seek to avoid commiting these offences and endeavor to get a reputation for what l is termed 'clean' fighting or sparring.

One of the things I invariably insist on in my classes is clean work. I will not tolerate a pupil that insists on perfecting himself in the art of fouling for some, indeed, have developed it to a point where it is unmistakably an art for the results are often very serious to the opponent, and aside from the bodily injury, he is done a great injustice. A man seldom expects a foul blow and consequently leaves unguarded the part of his body the hitting of which constitutes an unfair punch, and he does not keep on the lookout for other manceuvres equally as discreditable.

Every one knows that hitting below the belt is a foul and that practice is probably the most frequently committed blow of the class under consideration. It is nothing unusual to read of ring contests where a combatant loses through delivering a blow too low, and all boxers, amateur and professional alike, should exercise the greatest care in avoiding the landing of punches in the abdomen. True, sometimes a man will have his attacking hand struck down by his opponent in such a manner as to deflect it from its original direction to a part below the belt, but cases of this nature are entirely accidental and are not held against the man on the offensive by referee or witnesses.

Unfair Use of the Elbows

One common method of fouling is the bringing into play of the elbows. Sometimes in missing a blow for the face, say a hook or a jab, a man will double his arm as he lunges past his opponent and allow his sharp, bony elbow to strike. Then, again he will meet an opponent's rush with the forearm bent back and with the elbow point projecting to stop his man. You must be in close range to be met in this way, and when you unexpectedly come in against such a defence you can cause your contestant to regret his tactics by sending a left lead to his right ribs, or chopping your left over his right kidneys when he use his right elbow, or by shooting your right to his left ribs or heart, or chopping over his left kidney with your right when he uses his left elbow. You should endeavour to pin or block in some way your opponent's free hand with your disengaged fist. Otherwise he will be able to send it across to your face or body as he holds you off with his elbow. An 'elbow fighter' will generally try to implant his bent arm against your neck or chin when he stops an advance in this way. There are also times when boxers will use their elbows in breaking a clinch. When this is done you can counter with chops to either kidney with either hand as described in the foregoing paragraph.

Fouling with the Shoulder
Another foul blow is the using of the shoulder against the body of an opponent. By avoiding a lead for the head by ducking, a man will sometimes lunge forward, allowing his shoulder to strike on a man's ribs. When your lead is a straight one for the head with the left and your man drives his shoulder toward you, carry your right hand and forearm across your body, turning the hand outward and receiving the blow in the opened palm. During that proceeding your antagonist will have both hands free, but his crouching position in this instance will carry him so low as to render them practically useless for the time being.

Concerning Holding

A foul manoeuvre, which several fighters are prone to indulge in and which not infrequently gives them an advantage over a man, is that of eluding a lead and as it misses its mark securing the attacking hand and forearm between the elbow and the body. As the man is held in that position he is practically helpless. Many a well-laid plan of attack has been interrupted by the practice, and it often tends to make an opponent fear to deliver certain blows, as he will be in doubt as to whether he will again be awarded the same treatment.

Naturally you are at close quarters when your combatant works this trick on you, and you can often get in a short jab or hook to some open point before he can bring his free hand to the proper guarding position. Should he clutch your left lead for the body between his right elbow or upper arm and his ribs, send your right to the body or point of his chin, trying to avoid a block with his left; should he hold a straight right lead for the body to his opposite side in the same manner, your left, of course, will be the leading hand.

Always turn your head away from the side on which he clutches your lead, for if he is on the alert and knows the game well he will shoot his uplifted fist across your attacking arm to your head.

Many a fighter has been disqualified through resorting to the practice of holding as well as the other fouls I have mentioned, and so far as amateurs are concerned, they should not attempt to waste time and energy in dallying with unsanctioned features of the game. The professional boxer can sometimes afford to take the chances of fouling, for if he is very rapid in his movements he can 'get away' with the trick, but if he persists in the habit he will lose his reputation in a hurry. Admirers of fistiana, whether in a fifty-dollar box seat at the ringside, or in the loft of an old barn, like to see fair fighting, and as a general rule if they cannot get it they will stay at home and rock the cradle.

Maintain Your Rights
Always assert your own rights in a bout when you consider yourself to have been fouled, but do not drop your hands in the midst of an exchange of blows, for if, in the opinion of the referee, no offence has been committed, your opponent will thus be presented with a splendid opportunity to send you to the floor.

The question of foul blows has brought about many disputes in amateur as well as professional circles. Every one familiar with the sport remembers what was one of the most notable discussions of this sort, namely, that which arose on the Fitzsimmons–Sharkey bout at San Francisco several years ago. Sharkey was given the decision over the Cornishman through the

referee's believing that Bob hit Sharkey below
the belt. The sailor dropped to the floor after

the blow in question pressing his hands to his
stomach, and while his adherents were positive
that the punch was really a foul one, the backers
of Fitzsimmons were equally certain that it was

a perfectly allowable one. And so the matter stands to this day, and will stand till the end of time. Even now, spectators at the historic bout like to fight the battle over and tell how and why they formed their opinion either one way or the other.

Hints On Training

The man or youth anxious to become proficient in boxing should observe certain restrictions in his mode of living and while he is not required to hold himself so rigidly in line as do professional boxers he must conform to general regularity of habits, that is, of course, if he desires to obtain the full worth of the time and money expended.

To get into good condition requires strength of mind, for mankind is ever prone to lapse from uniform habits of living unless he has someone standing at hand with a rawhide lash to keep him in the straight and narrow way. But persevere. 'Stick-to-it-iveness' is developed only by long practice and the time is sure to come when you will experience no hardship whatever in confining yourself to regularity in eating, sleeping, exercising etc.

When the victory is finally won you will find yourself possessed of a strength of willpower you never before had and your acts in after life cannot help but show the effect of it to your advantage. In conditioning yourself the two things to which you should give most of your attention to are fresh air and plenty of exercise. Neither is of value without the other. All the exercise in the world will avail you nothing if it is carried on in a stuffy room with no ventilation, and naturally fresh air alone will never put strong muscles on your body. Keep out in the open every moment you can spare.

Diet and Breathing

Diet and a proper manner of breathing are also of great importrance. Your food should be chosen according to its intrinsic value as a nourishing element. Don't aim to be a lucullus if you wish to be a boxer, for a superabundance of rich foods and alcohoic drinks will nullify all the beneficial effects of your work by shortening your wind and making you fat and indolent. The lazy, slow-moving man might just as well cease to think seriously of boxing, for he is out of place in its immediate sphere.

Don't drink coffee. The nerves must be steady for boxing and when under pressure of an active opponent the coffee drinker will find his legs unsteady, the perspiration pouring from him and his blows will lack 'steam'.

As to the evils of alcoholic stimulants, I don't think I need add more to the hundreds of pages that have been written concerning them in their relation to athletics of all kinds. Ale or stout in moderate quantities at meal time will not harm you, but will give your system a desirable tone. Beer however, is very fattening and as for whiskey and brandy, they should be far removed from sparrers in every sense. Drink water, milk and weak tea without milk or sugar. Tobacco is another thing that should be tabooed. A cigar or two now and then will do no harm, but cigarettes, through the widespread tendency to inhale them, have a pernicious effect to say the least. They will ruin the soundest wind in a few days. Let them alone under all circumstances. Don't smoke cigarettes even if you never intend to indulge in any branch of athletics.

It is very strange, but nevertheless true, that the majority of people do not know how to breathe. Like all other athletes the boxer should lay special stress on this vital point. Too much time and trouble cannot be spent in perfecting yourself in the correct mode of inhalation and exhalation. A leading New York physician impressed me very forcibly once when he said, 'The average man or woman does not know when he is breathing.'

That is true. People go along day after day and never stop to consider that they are using but half of their breathing apparatus, a part of their bodies abnormally susceptible to disease when not in good condition and on which the measure of life they are to enjoy absolutely depends. Always take deep inhalations. Force the air down to the very bottom of your lungs and soon you will acquire the habit of so doing. Determine that you will know when you are breathing, regardless of other people who say, 'Well, I manage to get along all right, even if I do use but the top of my lungs.' Those foolish folk will never realize what really good health is until they change their short-sighted habit.

Exercises to Develop the Lungs

To develop your lungs so you will not become easily out of breath while boxing, set aside between fifteen to twenty minutes every morning and evening – just after rising and immediately before retiring for the following exercises:

Stand erect in the middle of the floor with the most of your clothing removed. Hold your arms straight at your sides with yours hands extended. Then draw them outward from the sides and upward, perfectly rigid, and draw in your breath gradually until the backs of the hands touch over your head, when the lungs should be absolutely full. Then let your hand drop gradually to your sides again, exhaling the while. The air in the lungs should be exhausted when the hand reach their original position. Repeat this movement a judicious number of times and vary it by extending the arms straight in front of you, the hands touching, and lifting them straight onr your head, bending backward at the waist as you do so. The inhaling and exhaling should be carried on as I before described. Frequently vary the rapidity of your arm movements and breathing. These exercises can be made more effective by holding light dumb bells in your hands as you raise them above your head. Your lung capacity can also be enlarged by standing erect, filling your lungs and then contracting rigidly the muscles of your hands, arms and chest and then bending forward and backward from the waist.

Do not hold in your breath too long while going through breathing exercises. If you do you will be likely to strain yourself injuriously, and besides there is no use in retaining vitiated air in the lungs longer than necessary. The blood depends for oxygen entirely on the fresh air brought into the lungs and if compelled to take in carbonic acid gas only harm can result, as you may readily observe.

Professional boxers are very abstemious when in training and when preparing for a contest their daily routine is an interesting study in hygiene. Their rules of life at the time are based on the teachings of actual experience and are laid down by men that have made a lifetime study of what is good or bad for athletes nearing a supreme test of their power. In order that every reader of this book may know just what their routine is and in the hope that they may derive

beneficial knowledge from a description of it
I will give a brief outline of the trained boxer's
life preliminary to a championship battle as it
has carried on under my observance.

How the Boxer Trains
The boxer in training rises around six o'clock
in the morning. He then goes through his
breathing exercises and goes out into the fresh,
early morning air for a walk or light run across
country or along a convenient road. He returns
around an hour later and after a bath and a
rubdown has breakfast. Bathing is an important
feature and after starting in with moderately
warm water he finishes with a cold shower
and a rub with rough towels. After breakfast
he goes out on the road for another walk, a
drive or perhaps a horseback ride, which gives
him a good appetite for dinner at twelve or half-
past. He always rests a bit before eating, never
putting food into his stomach when tired. His
dinner consists of lean beef or lamb or other
wholesome meats in moderation, a bottle of
ale or stout and a dessert of a simple nature,
say rice pudding or custard. He avoids starchy
vegetables and pastry and gives preference to
apple sauce, prunes, etc.

At half-past one or two o'clock he begins the
hardest work of the day. He spends time at the
wrist machine and the chest weights, swings
light Indian clubs and uses the dumb bells, skips

the rope, wrestles or 'roughs it' with a wrestling partner, spars at the punching bag from three to six three-minute rounds and boxes a few rounds with his sparring partner. The medicine ball is also brought into use and he finds admirable exercise in sparring at an imaginary opponent with dumb bells in his hands. This was a favorite pastime with Jim Corbett and a fine mode of developing the ability to do speedy work with the fists. The chest weights are splendid developers of the chest, shoulder and back muscles and in connection with the rowing attachment such as is used on the Spalding machine, form one of the best training machines I have ever seen. The rowing movement gives a highly desirable strength to the back, waist and thighs and at the same time promotes rather than retards suppleness.

The boxer retires about nine o'clock, after a quiet evening spent in reading the newspapers and in writing letters or talking. He must have eight hours sleep at least to keep him in the best shape and nothing is allowed to interrupt him when once he is in bed.

As the time for the bout approaches, the training is increased in severity until a few days before the great event, when nothing but the lightest kind of work is done. Strong efforts are made of course to prevent the man from 'going stale', and it is for this reason that the boxer's work is of so varied a nature. His mind must be kept occupied by thoughts of other things than himself and the approaching contest. In between his training intervals he will play baseball, go fishing if a stream is nearby, go to see a play in a nearby theater and do a score of other diverting things.

There is a great difference between modern and old-time training methods. The fighters of former days, especially when fights were frequently held in the open and bare hands used, also had primitive modes or preperation, which are now relegated to a back seat. Training then was intended to fit a man for long contests, from fifty to a hundred rounds and knockouts were unheard of, the men being literally worn to the ground by terrible punishment. Now the boxers are prepared to be speedy and accurate with the delivery of blows to the points where they will be most effective in the quickest time. In place of the old-time slugger we have the agile, eye pleasing, scientific boxer, and that it is a change for the better no impartial critic will deny.

The Way to Hit

How the Old-time Clever Men Did It

Chatting with a well-known boxer on the subject of the best way to hold the fist when hitting, I was surprised at learning that he always used his hands with the palms turned in. Small wonder knuckles are often knocked askew if there are many others who use their weapons in the same way. Clever men of the past, especially Peter Jackson, struck with the palm of the hand either up or down, and almost invariably bit with the back knuckles. The good judgment of this method was proved, in Jackson's case, by the fact that, despite his years of fighting and the resultant wear and tear of his armament, he went to his grave with every kuckle as sound as a hell. During an interview with a San Francisco newspaper man, George Green, a boxing instructor today, and a skillful exponent of the game of the ring when clever men were plentiful, had something like the following to say regarding hitting. Green, I might remark parenthetically, was such a master at his business that they dubbed him Young Corbett a distinct compliment, becausee Jim Corbett then filled the American public eye as a remarkable demonstrator of the science of pugilism.

'We're going back', declared Green,

> We don't even know how to hit. Go to a boxing show and you will see boys attempting to box with palm; held upward. Most of those boys have been tought to box that way. Look at the pictures of the old-time champions, and invariably you will find that they likewise held their fists palms upward. That was considered the proper way to box in their day. How in the world a man expected to put his full force into a blow delivered to the head of another when h is fist was in an unnatural position I cannot understand. My idea is to do things in the natural way. If you pick an object off a table you do it with palm down. And if you want to throw a ball as hard as you can, you certainly do not use the underhand delivery.

'Look,' said Green, and as he spoke he placed his doubled fist on a friend's jaw with the palm of the hand upward, 'now see if you can hit me on the face. Plunk! The friend landed. 'Now, don't imagine you are getting away with anything,' said Green. 'I wanted to show you how easy it was.' Then Green turned his hand with palm downward, 'now hit me,' he ordered. Again the friend slammed away. But this time he didn't land. Green's elbow and forearm blocked the way.

'That's the difference between the old way and the new,' he declared. 'When you hit at the face with the palm upward your own jaw is unprotected. Turn the palm down and you can put the full force into your blow, and at the same time establish a guard that the other fellow cannot break through unless he beats you to the punch.'

'Boxing, you understand,' continued Green,

Is a comparatively new art. The champions of the bare knuckle days were sluggers and not boxers. We have yet a lot to learn as to the tinier points. The history of real American boxing extends only to the time when Jim Corbett defeated John L. Sullivan at New Orleans in 1812. That was the first championship of America contest under Marquis of Queensberry rules.

Therefore it is not surprising that we still have a lot of the old fellows teaching boxing under methods that are not practicable in the modern game. These men were taught that the proper way to hold your hands was with palms upward. And few men can forget what they learned in their younger days. The proper way to hit is the way Jim Corbett did. We must give Corbett credit for a lot of things in connection with scientific boxing. Corbett received his first instruction from Walter Watson at the Olympic Club, San Francisco and not from De Witt Van Court, as it has been stated, so often.

But Watson had only the fundamental principles of boxing. He was an Englishman of the Jem Mace School. He gave Corbett the idea as to feinting and general footwork. Corbett improved on the idea, and within a very short time knew more than his teacher. Then when Watson retired instructor of the Olympic Club, and went into business, his place was taken by Corbett.

That marked the beginning of the new style of boxing. Corbett was its master. He dropped the hitting with palm upward and taught his pupils, of whom I was one, to hit with the palm down.

Rules Of Boxing

Amateur Athletic Union Rules

Section 1. In all boxing competitions the ring shall not be less than 16 feet nor more than 24 feet square, and shall be formed of knots and ropes, the latter extending in triple lines 2, 3 and 4 feet from the floor of the ring. The floor of the ring shall extend beyond the lower rope for a distance of not less than 2 feet. Posts must be properly padded and padding on floor shall be no less than half an inch in thickness.

Section 2. Competitors must box in regulation athletic trunks reaching to the knee, in shoes without spikes, or in socks, and use boxing gloves not less than 5 ounces in weight.

Section. 3. Classes to be 108 lbs and under, 115 lbs and under, 125 lbs and under, 135 lbs and under, 145 lbs and under, 158 lbs and under, 175 lbs and under, and over I5 lbs.

Section. 4. An athlete who fails to compete after entering an event shall be required to furnish a satisfactory excuse for such failure or render himself liable to censure or suspision by the local Registration Committee. Any athlete who weighs in and then fail; to compete without the excuse satisfactory to the registrarion committee shall be suspended for a period of six months. Competitors shall weigh in within three hours of a contest. Weighing-in shall cease in each class when the drawing for bouts in that class commences. Competitors shall sign their names to a weighing list upon weighing in and whenever demanded by the referee.

Section. 5. The Boxing Committee of each Association of the Amateur Athletic Union shall prepare an official list of competent boxing officials to serve as referees, judges, weighers, timers, ajudicaters, and clerks of boxing. All tournaments must be conducted by officials selected from this official list.

Section. 6. In all competitions the number of rounds to be contested shall be three. The duration of rounds shall be limited to three minutes each. The interval between each round shall be one minute. The referee may order one additional round as provided in Section IO.

Section. 7. A competitor failing to immediately respond to the call of 'time' at the beginning of any round shall he disqualified by the referee and the bout awarded to his opponent.

Section. 8. Immediately before the contest competitors who have weighed in shall draw numbers to determine the bouts they take part in. The contest to be as follows: Have the first preliminary round to reduce the number of competitors, to 2, 4, 8, 16, and so on.

(Thus if there are three competitors, have one preliminary bout to reduce to two; if five, have one bout to reduce to four; if six, have two bouts to reduce to four, if seven, have three bouts to reduce to four; if nine, have one bout to reduce to eight; if ten, have two bouts to reduce to eight; if eleven, have three bouts to reduce to eight, and so on.) In all drawings where numbers 1, 2, 3, 4 and so on are drawn, number 1 competes with number 2, 3 with 4 and so on. When the class is brought to a multiple of 2, 4, 8 or 16, the contest proceeds regularly to the final bout. The winner of the final bout receives first prize and the loser recieves second prize.

Section. 9. Each competitor shall be entitled to the assistance of two seconds only, and no advice or coaching shall he given to any competitor by either of his seconds, or by any other person during the progress of any round. For a violation of this section the referee may disqualify the competitor who is so advised or coached.

Section. 10. The manner of judging shall be as follows: There shall be two judges, stationed on opposite sides of the ring and a referee in the ring. At the end of the bout each judge shall write the name of the competitor who in his opinion has won and shall hand same to the announcer. In case the judges agree the name of the winner is announced, but in case the Judges disagree the announcer shall so inform the referee, who shall there upon himself decide. If the referee is in doubt he can order a further round limited to two minutes. If the judges then fail to agree the referee must decide in favour of one of the contestants.

Section. 11. The referee shall have power to caution or disqualify a competitor for any infringement of rules, and to end the round in the event of either man being knocked down. The referee however, shall not count over a competitor who has been knocked down. If such knockdown in his opinion shall incapacitate the competitor from continuing, the referee must stop the bout and announce the winner.

Section. 12. The decision of the judges or the referee, as the case may be, shall be final.

Section. 13. In all competitions the decision shall be made in favor of the competitor who displays the best style and obtains the greatest number of points. The points shall be as follows: For attack – direct clean hits with the knuckles of either hand, on any part of the front or sides of the head or body above the belt. For defense – guarding, slipping, ducking, counter-hitting or getting away. Where points are otherwise equal, consideration to be given to the man who does the most leading off.

Section. 14. The referee may disqualify a competitor who is boxing unfairly, by kicking, gouging or hitting with the open glove, hitting with the inside or butt of the hand, the wrist or elbow, hitting or catching hold below the waist, hitting when down (one knee and one hand or both knees on the floor), striking an opponrnt on the back of the neck or on the spine or over the kidneys, holding with one hand and striking, butting with the head or shoulder, hitting in the clinches, wrestling or roughing at the ropes, using offensive and scurrilous language, or not obeying the orders of the referee.

Section. 15. Any athlete who competes in a boxing contest of longer duration than provided for in these rules shall be suspended for such period as the Registration Committee shall decide.

Section. 16. Nothing shall be used for the protection of the hands and wrists other than soft cotton bandages of not more than three thicknesses and not more than two layers of tape back of the knuckles, hard bandages or substances of any kind being prohibited. Bandages are subject to approval of the referee.

Section. 17. In the event of any questions arising not provided for in these rules, the referee shall have full power to decide such questions and also to interpret the rules.

New York State Athletic Commission Rule

1. The boxing ring shall he constructed in a manner satisfactory to the Commission and shall not be less than 16 feet nor more than 24 feet square.

2. The scale of weights shall be:

	Pounds
Paperweight	108
Bantamweight	115
Featherweight	123
Lightweight	133
Welterweight	144
Middleweight	158
Commission	175
Heavy	all over

When boxers agree in their articles to make weight for a contest, the weight agreed upon must be at least six hours before ring time. All contestants must weigh in just before entering the ring, in the presence of the official inspector, regardless of private agreement or previous weighing.

3. The chief official of the boxing match or exhibition shall be the licensed referee, who must have a card from the Commission indentifying him as such, and no club shall employ or permit anyone to act excepting such officially licensed referees.

4. No decision shall be rendered by the referee. A decision may be given in amateur tournaments pursuant to the authority and jurisdiction of the Amateur Athletic Union.

5. Contestants must box in proper athletic costume, including protection cup.

6. Contestants may learn the name of the official referee of the club before whom they are to compete by application to the secretary of the Commission. If said contestants are not satisfied with the official referee they must notify the secretary of the Commission in writing forty-eight hours prior to the match or exhibition, and in case of failure to do so they must submit to the jurisdiction of the club referee.

7. All matches or exhibitions in which more than two principals appear in the ring at the same time, commonly called a 'battle royal' exhibition, are forbidden.

8. All clubs and contestants must enter into written contract, which contracts shall be executed in triplicate, each party holding one, the third copy to be mailed to the Commission immediately upon execution.

9. In all matches or exhibitions not more than four seconds shall attend or assist a contestant, and the official referee shall enforce said rule.

10. There shall be no coaching by the seconds or any other person, and the seconds must

remain seated during contest, and must not rise from their seats until the bell announces the termination of a round.

11. Chief or main match or exhibition shall commence not later than 10 p.m. The club must select from the various contestants the chief or main match or exhibition.

12. The kidney punch or blow shall be forbidden in all contests. The referee shall be sole judge of whether any other blow be fair or foul.

13. Only soft cotton or linen bandages shall be used, and all bandages shall be subject to the approval of the referee. Hard bandages or substances of any kind are prohibited.

14. No person under eighteen years of age shall he permitted to participate in any contest or exhibition.

15. Each contestant shall be examined prior to entering the ring, by a physician who has been licensed to practice in the State of New York for not less than five years. The physician shall certify in writing, over his signature, as to contestant's physical condition to engage in such contest. And said physician shall be in attendance during contest, prepared to deal with any emergency which may arise. Said physician shall file said report of examination with the Commission within a period of twenty-four hours after the contest. Blank forms

of physcian's reports may be had at the Commission's office, and all questions must be answered in full.

16. If a main match or exhibition is stopped by the referee, or by a member of the State Athletic Commission, or the secretary of the Commission, for an infraction of the rules of the Commission or for a violation of the provisins of Chapter 779 of the Laws of 1911, or the amendments thereto, the club shall hold all box office receipts of said match or exhibition for a period of forty-eight hours, pending the decision of the Commission.

17. No boxer shall be permitted to contest against an opponent ten pound s heavier than himself in the lightweight class or under said class.

18. Contests between negroes and white persons, otherwise known as mixed bouts, are strictly prohibited.

19. Introduct ions from the ring are limited to three individuals other than the contestants and referee.

20. Where boxers are working on a guarantee, the State Athletic Commission must be assured beyond a doubt as to the responsibility of the guarantor, otherwise the Commission will demand that the full amount of the guarantee he posted as directed by the Commission, not later

than 2 p.m., on the day preceding the contest. If the contest be on Monday, the guarantee must be posted at 11 a.m. on the Saturday preceding. Either contestant or the club must immediately notify the Commission, when, by any reason, a show or contest is declared off.

Unless the Commission be so notified before 2 p.m., on the day preceding the contest, suspension for at least thirty days will follow for the club or the party at fault. Any boxer causing a cancellation, must first fulfill his obligation to that club, or obtain a release from the club, before he will be permitted to box elsewhere.

Not more than forty rounds of boxing shall be scheduled at any one show, and every show must contain three four-round bouts and one six-round bout, except shows held under the auspices of the Amateur Athletic Union. No bout may be started after 11.15 p.m.

Marquis of Queensberry Rules
Rule 1 - To be a fair stand-up boxing match in a 24-foot ring, or as near that as practicable.

Rule 2 - No wrestling or hugging allowed.

Rule 3 - The rounds to be of three minutes' duration, and one minute between rounds.

Rule 4 - If either man fall, through weakness or otherwise, he must get up unassisted, ten seconds to be allowed him to do so, the other man meanwhile to return to his corner, and when the fallen man is on his legs the round is to be resumed and continued until the three minutes have expired. If one man fails to come to the scratch in the ten seconds allowed, it shall be in the power of the referee to give his award in favor of the other man.

Rule 5 - A man hanging on the ropes in a helpless state, with his toes off the ground, shall be considered down.

Rule 6 - No seconds or any other person to be allowed in the ring during the rounds.

Rule 7 - Should the contest be stopped by any unavoidable interference, the referee to name time and place, as soon as possible, for finishing the contest, so that the match must be won and lost, unless the backers of both men agree to draw the stakes.

Rule 8 - The gloves to be fair-sized boxing gloves of the best quality and new.

Rule 9 - Should a glove burst, or come off, it must be replaced to the referee's satisfaction.

Rule 10 - A man on one knee is considered down, and if struck is entitled to the stakes.

Rule 11 - No shoes or boots with springs allowed.

Rule 12 - Contest in all other respects to be governed by revised rules of London Prize Ring.

'Police Gazette' Revised Queensberry Rules
Rule 1 - The weights for all pugilists who contend in glove contests, according to the 'Police Gazette' boxing rules, shall be as follows - For heavyweights, over 158 lbs; middle, under 158 lbs and over 140 lbs; light, under 140 lbs.

Rule 2 - All contests to be decided in a 24 foot ring, which must be erected on the ground or stage.

Rule 3 - No wrestling or hugging allowed. The rounds to be of three minutes' duration and one minute time.

Rule 4 - Each contestant shall select an umpire, and they shall appoint a referee.

Rule 5 - In all contests two time-keepers shall be appointed, and the referee, under no circumstances, shall keep time.

Rule 6 - During the contest, if either man fall, through weakness or otherwise, he must get up unassisted, ten seconds being allowed him to do so, the other man meanwhile to retire to his corner; and when the fallen man is on his legs the round is to be resumed and continued until the three minutes have expired; and if one man fails to come to the scratch in the ten seconds allowed, it shall be in the power of the referee to give his award in favor of the other man.

Rule 7 - A contestant hanging on the ropes in a helpless state, with his toes off the ground, shall be considered down. No seconds, or any other person but the referee to be allowed in the ring.

Rule 8 - Should the contest be stopped by any unavoidable interference, the referee, if appointed, or else the stakeholder, shall name the next time and place for finishing the contest, as soon as possible, so that the match must he either won or lost.

Rule 9 - When either pugilist is knocked down within the allotted three minutes, he shall be allowed ten seconds to get on his feet again unassisted, except when this occurs in the last ten seconds.

Rule 10 - One minute's rest shall be allowed between each round, and no wrestling, roughing or struggling on the ropes shall be permitted.

Rule 11 - The gloves to be fair-sized boxing gloves, of the best quality and new. Should a glove burst or come off, it must be replaced to the referee's satisfaction. A man on one knee is considered down, and if struck is entitled to the stakes. No shoes or boots with spikes allowed.

Rule 12 - In all matches the stakes not to be open up untill won or lost by a fight. That if a man leaves the ring either to escape punishment or for any other purpose, with out the permission of the referee, unless he is involuntarily forced out, shall forfeit the battle.

Rule 13 - That any pugilist voluntarily quitting the ring, previous to the deliberate judgment of the referee being obtained, shall be deemed to have lost the fight.

Rule 14 - That the second shall not interfere, advise or direct the adversary of their principal, and shall refrain from all offensive and irritating expressions, in all respects conducting themselves with order and decorum, and confine themselves to the diligent and careful discharge of their duties to their principals.

Rule 15 - If either man shall wilfully throw himself down without receiving a blow, whether blows shall have been previously exchanged or not, he shall be deemed to have lost the battle; but that this rule shall not apply to a man who, in a close, slips down from the grasp of an opponent to avoid punishment or from obvious accident or weakness. The battle money shall remain in the hands of the stakeholder until fairly won or lost by a fight, unless a draw be mutually agreed upon, or in case of a postponement one of the principals shall be absent, when the man in the ring shall be awarded the stakes.

Rule 16 - A contest in which contestants agree to box four, six or a stipulated number of rounds, the referee shall have full power to order the men to continue, if it has not been decided during the four, six or number of rounds stipulated by one or the other of the pugilists stopping, losing by a foul or being beaten.

London Prize Ring Rules
Rule 1 - The ring shall be made on turf, and shall be 24-feet square, formed of eight stakes and ropes, the latter extending in double lines, the uppermost line being 4 feet from the ground, and the lower 2 feet from the ground. In the center of the ring a mark be formed, to be termed a scratch.

Rule 2 - Each man shall be attended to the ring by two seconds and a bottle-holder. The combatants, on shaking hands, shall retire until the seconds of each have tossed for choice of position, which adjusted, the winner shall choose his corner according to the state of the wind or sun, and conduct his man thereto, the loser taking the opposite diagonal corner.

Rule 3 - Each man shall be provided with a handkerchief of a color suitable to his own fancy, and the seconds shall entwine these hankerchiefs at the upper end of one of the centre stakes. These handkerchiefs shall be called 'colours', and the winner of the battle at its conclusion shall be entitled to their possession as the trophy of victory.

Rule 4 - The two umpires shall be chosen by the seconds or backers to watch the progress of the battle, and take exception to any breach of the rules herein after stated. A referee shall be chosen by the umpires, unless otherwise agreed on, to whom all disputes shall be referred; and the decision of this referee, whatever it may be, shall be final and strictly binding on all parties, whether as to the matter in dispute or the issue of the battle. The referee shall be provided with a watch for the purpose of calling time; the call of that referee only to be attended to, and no other person whatsoever shall interf ere in calling time. The referee shall withhold all opinion till appealed by the umpires, and the umpires strictly abide by his decision without dispute.

Rule 5 - On the men being stripped it shall be the duty of the seconds to examine their drawers, and if any objection arises as to insertion of improper substances therein, they shall appeal to their umpires, who, with the concurrence of the referee, shall direct what alterations shall be made.

Rule 6 - The spikes in the fighting boots shall be confined to three in number, which shall not exceed three-eighths of an inch from the sole of the boot, and shall not be less than one-eighth of an inch broad at the point; two to be placed in the broadest part of the sole and one in the heel; and in the event of a man wearing any other spikes, either in toes or elsewhere, he shall be compelled either to remove them or provide other boots properly spiked. The penalty for refusal to be a loss of the stakes.

Rule 7 - Both men being ready, each shall he conducted to that side of the scratch next his corner previously chosen; and the second on the one side and the men on the other, having shaken hands the former shall immediately leave the ring, and there remain until the round be finished, on no pretence whatever approaching their principals during the round, without permission from the referee. The penalty to be the loss of the battle to the offending parties.

Rule 8 - At the conclusion of the round when one or both of the men shall be down, the second shall step into the ring and carry or conduct their principal to his corner, there affording him the necessary assistance, and no person whatever be permitted to interfere in his duty.

Rule 9 - On the expiration of thirty seconds the referee appointed shall cry 'time', upon which each man shall rise from the knee of his second and walk to his own side of the scratch unaided, the seconds immediately leaving the ring. The penalty for either of them remaining eight seconds after the call of time to be the loss of the battle to his principal, and either man failing to be at the scratch within eight seconds shall be deemed to have lost the battle.

Rule 10 - On no consideration whatever shall any person except the seconds and the referee be permitted, to enter the ring during the battle, nor till it shall have been concluded, and in the eyent of such unfair practice, or the ropes or stakes being disturbed or removed, it shall be in the power of the referee to award the victory to that man, who, in his honest opinion, shall have the best of the contest.

Rule 11 - The seconds shall not interfere, advise or direct the adversary of their principal, and shall refrain from all offensive and irritating expressions, in all respects conducting themselves with order and decorum, and confine themselves to the diligent and careful discharge of their duties to their principals.

Rule 12 - In picking up their men, should the second wilfully injure the antagonist of their principal, the latter shall be deemed to have forfeited the battle on the decision of the referee.

Rule 13 - It shall be a fair 'stand-up fight', and if either man shall wilfnlly throw himself down without receiving a blow, whether blows shall have been previously exchanged or not, he shall be deemed to have lost the battle, but this rule shall not apply to a man who in a close slips down from the grasp of his opponent to avoid punishment, or from obvious accident or weakness.

Rule 14 - Butting with the head shall be deemed foul, and the party resorting to this practice shall be deemed to have lost the battle.

Rule 15 - A blow struck when a man is thrown or down shall be deemed foul. A man with one knee and one hand on the ground or with both knees on the ground, shall be deemed down; and a blow given in either of these positions shall be considered foul, providing always that, when in such position, the man so down shall not himself strike, or attempt to strike.

Rule 16 - A blow struck below the waistband shall be deemed foul, and in a close, seizing an antagonist below the waist, by the thigh or otherwise shall be deemed foul.

Rule 17 - All attempts, to inflict injury by gouging, or tearing the flesh with the fingers or nails, and biting shall be deemed foul.

Rule 18 - Kicking, or deliberately falling on an antagonist, with the knees or otherwise when down, shall be deemed foul.

Rule 19 - All bets shall be paid as the battle money after a fight is awarded.

Rule 20 - The referee and umpires shall take their positions in front of the centre stake, outside the ropes.

Rule 21 - Due notice shall be given by the stakeholder of the day and place where the battle money is to he given up, and be exonerated from all responsibility upon obeying the direction; the referee: all parties be strictly bound by these rules; and in future, all articles of agreement for a contest be entered into with a strict and willing adherence to the letter and spirit of these rules.

Rule 22 - In the event of magisterial or other interference, or in case of darkness coming on the referee (or stakeholder in case no referee has been chosen) shall have the power to name the time and place for the next meeting, if possible on the same day, or as soon after as may be. In naming the second or third place the nearest split shall be selected to the original place of fighting where there is a chance of its being fought out.

Rule 23 - Should the fight not be decided on the day all bets shall be drawn, unless the fight shall be resumed the same week, between Sunday and Sunday, in which case the referee's duties shall continue and the bets shall stand and be decided by the event. The battle money shall remain in the hands of the stakeholder until fairly won or lost by a fight, unless a draw be mutually agreed upon, or in case of a postponement, one of the principals shall be absent, when the man in the ring shall be awarded the stakes.

Rule 24 - Any pugilist voluntarily quitting the ring previous to the deliberate judgment of the referee being obtained shall be deemed to have lost the fight.

Rule 25 - On an objection being made by the seconds or umpire the men shall retire to their corners, and there remain until the decision of the appointed authorities shall be obtained; if pronounced 'foul' the battle shall be at an end, but if 'fair', 'time' shall be called by the party appointed, and the man absent from the scratch in eight seconds after shall be deemed to have lost the fight. The decision in all cases to be given promptly and irrevocably, for which purpose the umpire; and the referee shall be invariably close together.

Rule 26 - If a man leaves the ring, either to escape punishment or for any other purpose, without the permission of the referee, unless he is involuntarily forced out, shall forfeit the battle.

Rule 27 - The use of hard substances, such as stones or sticks, or of resin in the hand during the battle shall be deemed foul, and on the requisition of the seconds of either man, the accused shall open his hands for the examination of the referee.

Rule 28 - Hugging on the ropes shall he deemed foul. A man held by the neck against the stakes or upon or against the ropes shall be considered down, and all interference with him in that position shall be foul. If a man in any way makes use of the ropes or stakes to aid him in squeezing his adversary he shall be deemed the loser of the battle, and if a man in a close reaches the ground with his knees, his adversary shall immediately loose him or lose the battle.

Rule 29 - All glove or room fights be as nearly as possible in conformity with foregoing rules.

The correct boxing position.

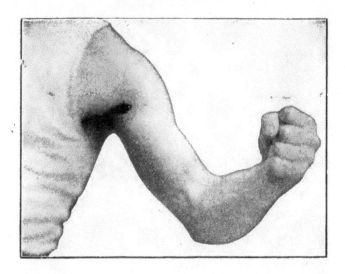

Clinching the fist – the proper way, holding thumb below line of middle finger joints.

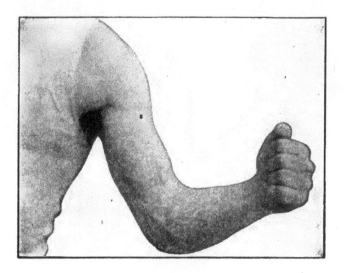

Clinching the fist – the improper way. Note position of thumb.

Sparring for an opening.

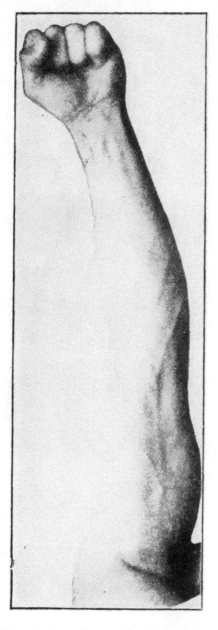

Position of hand and arm for straight left to the face.

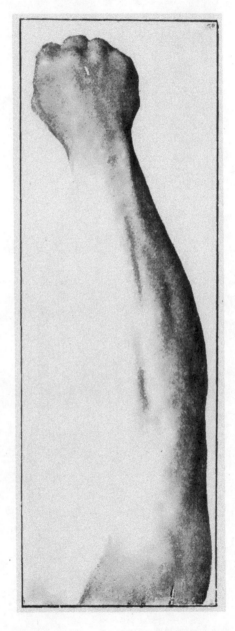

Position of hand and arm for right to face or body.

Position for left-hand jab to the face. Left lead to the face and counter to the body.

Slipping a straight left for the head (a double slip).

Blocking a left lead to the body and countering with left hook to the face.

Crouching and sending the left straight to the body.

The right-hand cross-counter to the head.

Slipping a right-hand cross-counter to the head.

Slipping a straight right lead for the face and countering with a left swing to the body.

Drawing away from a right swing to counter with straight
right to face.

Shifting from a straight left lead to head and countering with right to body.

Shoving aside opponent's left lead with your right and
countering to body with left.

Blocking a left swing to body and delivering a short left swing to face.

Slipping a straight left lead to head and delivering a left-hand uppercut to body.

The corkscrew blow.

Ducking a left swing and countering to the body with a left swing.

Pinning your opponent's right with your left and delivering a
right hook to jaw.

The liver punch.

Ducking a right-hand swing and getting in position to send
either hand to body.

Blocking an opponent's high left swing for the head and standing ready to block his right jab to body.

Foul blows Holding an attacking hand between elbow and body.

Jess Willard, Champion of the World.

Georges Carpentier, French and English Heavyweight
Champion (Copyright by American Press Association).

1, Chip saves himself from falling; 2, Darcy's left in evidence (vs. Clabby); 3, Darcy leads the left; 4, Clabby 'smothers' from Darcy's attack with left; 5, Clabby ducks from a right by Darcy. Scenes in Les Darcy's Contests in Australia with Jimmy Clabby and George Chip.

The CLASSIC GUIDE

TO DATING

HENRY J. WEHMAN

978-1-4456-4419-6

THE CLASSIC GUIDE

TO

COCKTAILS

JERRY THOMAS

978-1-4456-4726-5

The Classic Guide to POLO

T. F. DALE

978-1-4456-4866-8

The
Classic Guide
to
FLY FISHING

H. CHOLMONDELEY-PENNELL

978-1-4456-4723-4

The

Classic Guide
to
ATHLETICS

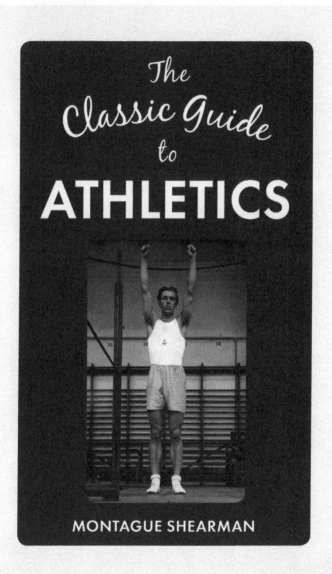

MONTAGUE SHEARMAN

978-1-4456-4483-7